Bicycling
Salt Lake City

A Guide to the Best Mountain and
Road Bike Rides in the Salt Lake City Area

Gregg Bromka

FALCONGUIDES®

GUILFORD, CONNECTICUT
HELENA, MONTANA

AN IMPRINT OF THE GLOBE PEQUOT PRESS

*A*FALCONGUIDE ®□

Falcon and FalconGuides are registered trade-
marks of Morris Book Publishing, LLC.

Maps by Multi-Mapping Ltd. © Morris Book
Publishing, LLC.
Photo credits: p.15 by Brand X; p. 69 by Dave
Iltis.

Library of Congress Cataloging-in-Publication
Data is available.
ISBN 978-0-7627-4096-3

Manufactured in the United States of America
First Edition/First Printing

Contents

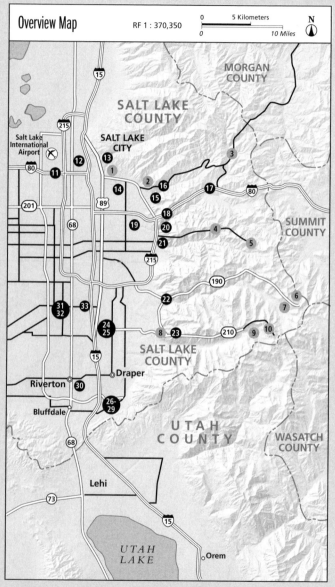

Overview Map

RF 1 : 370,350

0   5 Kilometers

0   10 Miles

N

MORGAN COUNTY

SALT LAKE COUNTY

Salt Lake International Airport

SALT LAKE CITY

SUMMIT COUNTY

Salt Lake County

Draper

Riverton

Bluffdale

UTAH COUNTY

WASATCH COUNTY

Lehi

UTAH LAKE

Orem

① Mountain Biking Ride Location   ⑪ Road Biking Ride Location

MAP LEGEND

Boundaries

/////	National Park/Wildlife
— ·· — ··	County

Transportation

—(15)—	Interstate
—(89)—	U.S. Highway
—(65)—	State Highway
—	Road
(P)	Paved
(G)	Gravel (improved)
= = = = = :	Unimproved

Rides

·-·-·-·-·	Road Ride
- - - - -	Mountain Ride
- - - - - -	Other Ride
——	Ski Lift/Tram
/	Change in Trail Surface
(S)	Singletrack
(D)	Doubletrack

Degree of Difficulty

●	Easy
□	Moderate
◆	Difficult

Hydrology

~~	Rivers/Creeks
▬	Lake

Symbols

♠	Accommodations
∴	Archaeological/Ruin

⊛	Bicycles Prohibited
⏝	Bridge/Overpass
☕	Cafe
△	Campground
♟	Cemetery
✝	Church
⒜	Communication Tower
•—•	Gate
⛳	Golf Course
⚔	Gravel pit
✚	Hospital
■	Important Building
❓	Information
⊗	International Airport
✤	Marina
▮	Monument
▲	Mountain/Peak
⏛	Museum
邢 ♟	Park
★	Point of Interest
🍴	Restaurant
♟	School
⛿	Shopping Center
⊔	Stadium
🏛	State Capitol
⑬ 🚲	Trailhead
)——(	Tunnel
✆	University
⌷	UTA Trax Station
◉	Viewpoint

Foreword

I was excited to learn that Gregg was writing this guide-book, *Bicycling Salt Lake City*. Since 1983 I have been regularly riding in the Salt Lake Valley. During that time I have carved out many routine rides. In doing so, I have often thought, "Someone should write a book on bicycle routes in Salt Lake." Finally, Gregg has done that.

Salt Lake is absolutely one of the finest urban areas in which to ride. I have made it a practice to take my bike with me when I travel. I have ridden in Boston, Quebec, Washington, D.C., Portland (Oregon), San Diego, Montreal, and many other urban areas. Salt Lake is as good as the best of these. Like any urban area, though, you have to get to know it, or you need a good guide.

Gregg's guidebook focuses on road riding, but he has included ten classic mountain bike rides to provide a comprehensive, all-around guide to the Salt Lake Valley. The road riding guide has been sorely needed. Meanwhile, Gregg has already written, in addition to numerous others, a mountain biking guidebook that covers the entire Wasatch Range, *Mountain Biking Utah's Wasatch Front*.

While I enjoy mountain biking as much as anyone, a mountain bike ride is more of an excursion. I have long recognized that road biking has the huge advantage of rolling right out of my garage for a good ride. Right from home (or apartment or hotel), one can get in a daily ride in a minimum amount of time almost every day of the week, or escape for a long ride. And the car stays put.

One of the primary benefits of *Bicycling Salt Lake City* is that the routes will be, as much as possible, bicycle friendly. In an urban area that becomes a big factor, as many people are frightened from riding because of the fear of traffic, and the routes in this book attempt to mitigate such fears.

I was pleased to find that many of these routes mirror the ones I created for myself or learned from others over the years. This is not surprising, as knowledge of good routes tends to circulate among long-time resident riders. This guidebook will, nevertheless, introduce most seasoned cyclists to new routes and will be a valuable possession for visitors and for those who recently have or will take up bicycling.

Bicycling Salt Lake City caters to riders of all skill, strength, and endurance levels. From an easy ride on the Jordan River Parkway, to a climb up Little Cottonwood Canyon that rivals some of the toughest Tour de France climbs, to a long century around the Oquirrh Mountains, this guidebook provides something for everyone.

Gregg has written a regular column on Utah mountain bike rides for *cycling utah,* the region's long-standing cycling publication. As the publisher, I have always appreciated Gregg's contributions and found them to be concise, with directions that are easily followed and descriptions that are easily understood. He brings his professional talent and experience to this book.

Salt Lake is a great place to ride. It has been home to numerous great cyclists, including 2005 Tour de France yellow jersey holder David Zabriskie; Tour contender Levi Leipheimer; former professional cyclist and Tour rider Marty Jemison; junior mountain biking World Champion Jeff Osguthorpe; and Masters World Champions Steve Johnson.

Beyond that, Salt Lake is home to thousands of cyclists of all varieties and levels. For all these and the valley's many visitors, *Bicycling Salt Lake City* will be a welcome asset.

—David R. Ward, publisher of *cycling utah*

Preface

When I was first approached to write this book, I was skeptical. For nearly twenty years now I have been a mountain biking purist and have been caught up in the wave of popularity that has seized mountain biking. My love for riding on dirt inspired me to write numerous guidebooks, including *Mountain Biking Utah's Wasatch Front* and *Mountain Biking Utah*. But a guide to Salt Lake's road bike rides? Who would want that?

Don't get me wrong. I ride a road bike as well, and I am intimately familiar with the Wasatch canyons from City Creek to Little Cottonwood. I know that the MS 150 and Cycle Salt Lake Century draw big crowds and that the road racing scene is alive in Utah. But does the local road cycling community have the depth and following of the Red Bull–slurping fat-tire culture? My question was answered with resounding confirmation one fall morning.

While nursing a nagging back injury, I heard the whir of bicycles passing my home. (I happen to live on a popular east-side bike route.) I expected to see a small pack of jersey-clad racers logging training miles. On the contrary, my eyes fell upon a scene that was downright shocking. For as far as I could see down the road, a line of more than *one thousand* cyclists were making their way past my home en route to Big Cottonwood Canyon, all led by 2005 Tour de France stage winner, and local, Dave Zabriskie. It was the second annual Josie Johnson Memorial Ride. Whoa! I stood alongside the road for ten minutes bug-eyed and with mouth agape while vicariously joining the ranks. And I'm sure there were a thousand or more who didn't or couldn't make the J.J. ride. "Roadies rule," I mused, and I dove head-long into this project.

The canyons of the central Wasatch Range are classic climbs, but riding the roads throughout Salt Lake County is more than gut-wrenching, leg-searing ascents. I quickly discovered that there are countless miles of quality road routes across the entire valley. Some require a well-tuned power plant, whereas others are mellow flights that are just right for fledglings. Some take you to the far reaches of the county and others curve through quaint neighborhoods. The result is a countywide cross section of road routes that cater to riders of all abilities.

Although the focus of this guidebook is road rides, I am unable to turn my back on my penchant for dirt, so I've included ten of the best mountain bike trails in the central Wasatch Range. Like the current wave of popular vehicles, this book has become a "crossover" guide that strives to unite the entire bicycling community.

To all who pedal on two wheels, you're kindred spirits.

Introduction

Time and again, postcards and travel brochures of Salt Lake City depict a compact business skyline backed by tall, rugged mountains that appear as though they might topple down onto the city below. The photographs look contrived, made up, with mountains and buildings juxtaposed for effect. But they are real, for nestled at the base of the Wasatch Range, which rises sharply more than a vertical mile above the valley floor, Salt Lake City is a geographic wonderland and is shockingly beautiful. It was the "right place" for Brigham Young and his Mormon Pioneers when they trekked across the country and entered the Salt Lake Valley in 1847, and it's the right place today if your penchant is for riding a bicycle.

If you make your way up to Wasatch Boulevard on the valley's eastern foothills, you can take in the entire 35-mile-long, 13-mile-wide Salt Lake Valley, wedged neatly between the Wasatch Range on the east and the Oquirrh Mountains to the west. The valley is home to nearly one million residents. More boggling is the countless miles of roadways that stretch across the valley floor, laid out to perfection like the circuits on a microchip. Now, spin around and tilt your head up at the Wasatch Range. Behind that seemingly impervious wall of rock are deeply cut canyons, lush basins, and treeless peaks that harbor some of the sweetest sinuous dirt tracks known. Like a famished dog eyeing a juicy bone, you'll salivate over the cycling opportunities that await you, and you'll savor the tender marrow of that bone in *Bicycling Salt Lake City.*

About this Guide

Bicycling Salt Lake City is for the total bicyclist, one who embraces both the skinny- and fat-tire elements of bicycling. Why limit yourself? Mountain biking frees you from the confines of urbanism, but it often takes the ultimate end product of urbanism to get you to the trailhead. Road riding, on the other hand, captures the very essence of freedom of escape. Simply open the door, clip into the pedals, and escape on your bike. You can do both in Salt Lake City, and that's what you'll find in this guidebook.

Elliot Mott nailed it on the head when, in the early 1990s, he titled his series of local road biking books *Cycling Possibilities.* Like Mott's books, *Bicycling Salt Lake City* offers a myriad of road biking possibilities throughout the Salt Lake Valley— twenty-three in all—tallying nearly 600 miles. Rather than regurgitate the same information, *Bicycling Salt Lake City* takes a fresh look at the many classic road bike routes by steering you onto newly favored lanes and away from old, soured roads. You'll find several never-before-published routes, too, as new roadways have since been developed through new communities and to new destinations.

Salt Lake City continually plays second fiddle to mountain biking hot spots like Moab, Durango, and British Columbia, and big metros like Denver, San Francisco, and New York City get more press. Perhaps the trails of the central Wasatch Range are the nation's best-kept secret. Salt Lake's big-city offerings, high quality of life, varied seasons, and proximal mountain trails border on perfection overall.

The ever-expanding Bonneville Shoreline Trail is anchored in Salt Lake City and offers nearly year-round riding. As snow melts and summer arrives, the Wasatch Range beckons mountain bikers to tickle its singletracks with their knobby tires. Use Mill Creek Pipeline Trail, Big Water Trail, and Mormon Pioneer Trail to gauge the progress of your ability throughout the season. Then roll out onto the Wasatch Crest Trail for a ride on the area's premier single-track across the top of the namesake mountains. Even the area's ski resorts get into the action. Solitude Mountain Resort and Snowbird Resort offer lift service for gravity lovers, whereas Alta Ski Area opens its Albion Basin Summer Road for a mellow jaunt into the heart of classic ski terrain.

On the valley floor rides were carefully chosen for their location and attraction. You'll find many routes for building your fitness, where you can spin over nearly flat or gently rolling terrain. How about riding 30 miles with barely 50 feet of elevation gain? We're not talking about the corn-fields of Kansas but the ride to Saltair. Along the Wasatch foothills, routes like the Dimple Dell Loop combine hills and flats as they flirt between the elevated benches and the valley floor. And then there are the famed Wasatch canyons, which range from the mild-mannered Emigration Canyon Road to the gut-wrenching Little Cottonwood Canyon Road. Got legs? Whether you ride solo, lead a group, or are part of the peloton, you'll find great and varied road riding in Salt Lake City.

Keep in mind that not one road bike ride presented in this guide is the final word on how it should be ridden. If you follow these routes verbatim, you'll have a great ride, but odds are you'll log into many rides at different locations than the suggested trailheads and cut out from the courses at points other than the rides' suggested ends. Or, more often than not, you'll tweak a ride by linking it to adjoining routes to meet your ride objectives of distance and difficulty. If you ask ten cyclists how they ride the Cotton Bottom Loop (also know as the Josie Johnson Memorial Ride), you'll likely get ten different answers because there are countless variations on the theme. That's the beauty of riding in Salt Lake and the concept behind this book. Individual rides were purposefully kept short, 30 miles or less, to cater to a wide range of cyclists. Only your physical ability will limit your creativity for combining routes into longer tours. If you look to the end of the ride mileage logs, you'll find tips on how to expand your "cycling possibilities."

Whether you're a resident or a visitor, a rookie or a seasoned veteran, saddle up and come along for the ride. In no time you'll agree that Salt Lake City is one of the sweetest big-city locales for bicycling. Mum's the word!

Getting Involved

Bicycling Salt Lake City is but one of many resources that a bicyclist can turn to for valuable road and trail information. For a "one-stop-shopping" approach to all things bicycling, pick up a copy of *cycling utah,* which is available for free at most bike shops, sporting goods stores, book stores, and libraries. Here's a list of other cycling resources:

- Salt Lake City's Mayor's Bicycle Advisory Committee *(Salt Lake City Bikeways Map):* www.slcgov.com/ transportation/bicycle/MBAC.htm
- Salt Lake County Bicycle Advisory Committee (Salt Lake County Bike Map): www.slcbac.org
- Utah Bicycle Coalition (Utah bicycle/roadway laws): www.utahbike.org
- Critical Mass (monthly mass ride): www.slccritical mass.org

- Cycle Salt Lake Week and Cycle Salt Lake Century (mid-May): www.cyclesaltlakecentury.com
- Salt Lake City Bicycle Collective (bicycling community outreach): www.slcbikecollective.org
- Bonneville Bicycle & Tandem Club (day rides and multiday-tours): www.bbtc.net
- Utah Cycling Association (local branch of USA Cycling): www.utahcycle.com
- Wasatch Mountain Club (weekly road and mountain bike rides): www.wasatchmountainclub.org
- Public Lands Information Center (recreation information specialists located in REI, Salt Lake): (801) 466-6411
- Bonneville Shoreline Trail Committee: www.bonneville-trail.org
- Salt Lake Ranger District, Wasatch-Cache National Forest: www.fs.fed.us/r4/wcnf/unit/slrd/index/shtml
- Intermountain Cup Mountain Bike Race Series: www.intermountaincup.com
- *Mountain Biking Utah's Wasatch Front* (Off-Road Publications): www.offroadpub.com

Rules of the Trail

Trail etiquette is a subject that cannot be overemphasized. Your every action as a mountain biker has an impact on the trail, on the environment, and on how you are perceived by others. Follow the Rules of the Trail established by the International Mountain Bike Association (IMBA):

1. Ride on open trails only. Respect trail and road closures (ask if uncertain), avoid trespassing, and obtain necessary permits.

2. Practice zero impact. Be sensitive to the dirt beneath you. Avoid riding on wet and muddy trails. Don't cut switchbacks and stay on designated trails. Pack out what you pack in.

3. Control your bicycle. Inattention for even a second can cause problems. Obey bicycle speeds and regulations.

4. Always yield the trail. Let your fellow trail users know you're coming with a friendly greeting or bell. Pass at a walking pace. Slow down and anticipate trail users around blind corners.

5. Never scare animals. A sudden unannounced approach can startle animals, which can be dangerous. Use special care when passing horses and ask the horseback rider for instructions on how to pass.

6. Plan ahead. Be self-sufficient, keep your equipment in good repair, pack necessary repair tools, and carry adequate food and water. Always wear a helmet and appropriate safety gear.

Remember this one point every time you ride: Just because you *can* doesn't mean you *should!*

Rules of the Road

We've all been there. A motorist cuts you off and barks a few choice words out the car window, and you hoist the proverbial finger flag. You mull over and over, "I have rights!" And you *do* have many of the same rights to the road as motorists do. But as Riley Butler of Wasatch Touring is quick to note, there is a huge difference between being right and being *dead* right! Exercise your rights to the road, but do so prudently. For a list of Utah bicycle laws, visit the Utah Bicycle

Coalition Web site (www.utahbike.org/resources.html) and follow these common sense rules:

1. Ride properly equipped. Wear a helmet and brightly colored clothes. Use headlights and taillights when riding at night. Carry adequate food and water and pack along repair equipment.

2. Use hand signals. Point an outstretched arm in the direction you intend to turn and signal well in advance.

3. Go with the flow. Ride in the same direction as traffic and as far right as practical. When conditions warrant, you are permitted to ride in the center of the traffic lane. By law motorists must leave 3 feet when passing a bicyclist.

4. Obey traffic signs and signals. Bicycles must be driven like other motor vehicles and obey all traffic laws. Do not run red lights or stop signs.

5. Choose the best way to turn left. Use left-turn lanes when available or cross at crosswalks with pedestrians.

6. Avoid hazards. Watch out for storm drains, road striping, gravel, ice, parked cars, etc., in your path and avoid making sudden maneuvers to avoid hazards.

7. Go slow on sidewalks. Pedestrians have the right of way on walkways. Give an audible warning when passing pedestrians.

8. Ride defensively. Assume motorists do not see you and anticipate possible situations that could lead to an accident.

9. Park and lock your bike. Buy the best lock you can afford and lock both wheels and the frame to a bike rack or immovable object.

How to Use This Guide

Most of the information in this book is self-explanatory, but if anything in a ride description doesn't make sense, then reread the following explanation of the format. The information is listed in an at-a-glance format as follows:

The **ride number** refers to where the ride falls in this guide. Use this number when cross-referencing between rides and for finding rides on the overview map.

Start tells where the ride is located in the greater Salt Lake Valley or Wasatch Range.

Distance gives the ride's length in miles. Configuration is also noted: loop, one-way, out-and-back, or a combination of these.

Gain gives the total amount of climbing in feet for the entire route.

Physical difficulty estimates the physical challenge of the ride. The levels are easy, moderate, and strenuous. Keep in mind that the difficulty of a ride is relative to Salt Lake City and the Wasatch Range and may vary significantly from the difficulty of rides in other locations.

Easy rides are mostly flat but may include some rolling hills. Any climbs will be short.

Moderate rides will have climbs; some may be steep. Strenuous sections may occur but are generally short in duration.

Strenuous rides are long hauls on flatter terrain, short rides with numerous steep climbs, or long rides with numerous or continuous steep climbs.

Technical difficulty (mountain biking) rates the trails' roughness and the level of bike-handling skill needed to ride the trail without "dabbing" (touching the foot down) or dismounting. Ratings are 1 to 1+ for a smooth dirt road, 2 to 2+ for smooth doubletracks or singletracks, 3 to 3+ for lightly rutted or rocky doubletracks and singletracks, 4 to 4+ for very rough and rocky doubletracks and singletracks, and 5 to 5+ for extremely rough trails with severe gradients.

Margin of comfort (road biking) addresses the overall safety level of a road for bicycling, considering traffic volume, traffic speed, shoulder width, intersections, and pavement quality. Levels are poor, fair, and good. Margin of comfort might change often throughout a ride because the above-noted conditions might change. Margin of comfort is subjective and should be used as a rough guideline for route selection.

Trail surface (mountain biking) describes the type of path you ride on. A *singletrack* is a narrow one-lane dirt path that might or might not be maintained. A *doubletrack* is an unimproved dirt road consisting of dual parallel lanes, usually separated by a raised berm of dirt or grass, i.e., a "jeep road." A high-clearance vehicle with four-wheel drive may be required. A *dirt road* is a light-duty dirt road or an all-weather gravel road that is generally suitable for passenger cars when dry, but may require four-wheel drive when wet. A *paved road* is any secondary, primary, or interstate roadway.

Season tells you at what time of the year the ride is most enjoyable or is practical.

Land status (mountain biking) describes the ownership of the land the trail crosses and/or what government agency or agencies oversee the trail.

Maps lists the USGS maps that cover the route in either 1:24,000 scale (7.5-minute topographic quadrangle) or 1:100,000 scale (metric). Other pertinent maps may be listed.

Finding the trailhead tells you how to drive to the ride's trailhead (mountain biking) or to the suggested starting point (road riding). You might be able to start a road ride from other locations.

Know before you go offers important notes, precautions, and/or unusual hazards that pertain to the route, along with fees, regulations, and/or restrictions.

The Ride presents the mile-by-mile, turn-by-turn narrative that may be necessary for you to complete the ride without getting misdirected or lost, heaven forbid. A painstaking attempt has been made to accurately describe every route. Be aware that it is unlikely that bicycle computers on different bikes will yield the same mileages. Still, the mileages presented should help you gauge your progress for a safe ride. Additional notes may follow this section to offer more information or to give you insight on how to vary the described route.

The **elevation profile** shows the route's distance, change in elevation and tread surface, and key landmarks or turns. For mountain bike trails, changes in general technical difficulty ratings are shown on a scale of 1 to 5, as noted above. For road rides, changes in general margin of comfort are shown: P, poor; F, fair; and G, good.

The **maps** are clean, easy-to-use navigational tools. Not all trails or roads may be shown, nor all trail junctions or intersections. Still, a painstaking effort was made to include pertinent information for a safe, easily navigated ride.

Rides at a Glance

Mountain Biking Rides

Beginner's Luck (easy to moderate)
4. Mill Creek Pipeline Trail, 7.2 miles
10. Albion Basin Summer Road, 6 miles
5. Big Water Trail, 6.4 miles

Kick It Up a Notch (moderate to strenuous)
8. Little Cottonwood Canyon Trail, 6.4 miles
2. Bonneville Shoreline Trail (Salt Lake City), 10 miles
1. Bonneville Shoreline Trail (Ensign Peak), 11.2 miles
3. Mormon Pioneer Trail, 6.8 miles
6. Wasatch Crest Trail, 15.2 miles

Gravity Games (lift access)
7. Solitude Mountain Resort, distance varies
9. Snowbird Resort, distance varies

Early and Late Season
1. Bonneville Shoreline Trail (Ensign Peak), 11.2 miles
2. Bonneville Shoreline Trail (Salt Lake City), 10 miles
4. Mill Creek Pipeline Trail, 7.2 miles
8. Little Cottonwood Canyon Trail, 6.4 miles

Prime Time (midseason)
3. Mormon Pioneer Trail, 6.8 miles
5. Big Water Trail, 6.4 miles
6. Wasatch Crest Trail, 15.2 miles
7. Solitude Mountain Resort, distance varies
9. Snowbird Resort, distance varies
10. Albion Basin Summer Road, 6 miles

Road Biking Rides

Flat as a Pancake (easiest to hardest)

31. Jordan River Parkway, distance varies
12. North Salt Lake Loop, 20.5 miles
27. Draper Loop, 14.2 miles
11. Saltair, 31.4 miles
32. West Jordan–Bluffdale Loop (the "Pen" Loop), 24.1 miles
30. Camp Williams Loop, 27.3 miles
29. Draper-Herriman Loop, 25.1 miles

The East Bench (easiest to hardest)

15. Bonneville Shoreline Trail (Parleys Crossing), 8.4 miles
24. Sego Lily Drive Loop, 8.1 miles
26. Dimple Dell Loop (Sandy), 14.5 miles
25. Dimple Dell Loop (Draper), 12.3 miles
16. Josie Johnson Memorial Ride, 20.2 miles
17. Wasatch Boulevard, 21.8 miles
28. Traverse Mountains Loop, 24.5 miles
14. Bountiful Bench, 29.2 miles

Classic Canyons (easiest to hardest)

18. Emigration Canyon Road, 15.6 miles
13. City Creek Canyon Road, 11.2 miles
19. East Canyon Road, 16.2 miles
20. Parleys Canyon/I–80, 22 miles
21. Mill Creek Canyon Road, 18.8 miles
22. Big Cottonwood Canyon Road, 29.4 miles
23. Little Cottonwood Canyon Road, 17.4 miles

The Real Deal

33. Oquirrh Mountains Loop, 102 miles

Supersize It (classic combos; miles are approximate)

- Emigration Canyon + Parleys Canyon/I-80 (exit 134) + Bonneville Shoreline Trail (Parleys Crossing), 21 miles
- Draper Loop + Dimple Dell Loop (Draper), 24 miles
- Parleys Canyon/I-80 + East Canyon Road, 26 miles
- Emigration Canyon Road + East Canyon Road, 31 miles
- Bountiful Bench (loop portion) + North Salt Lake Loop, 34 miles
- Wasatch Boulevard + Dimple Dell Loop (Draper), 35 miles
- Draper Loop + Traverse Mountain Loop, 35 miles
- West Jordan–Bluffdale Loop + Camp Williams, 35 miles
- West Jordan–Bluffdale Loop + Draper-Heriman Loop, 35 miles
- Wasatch Boulevard + Dimple Dell Loop (Sandy), 36 miles
- Parleys Canyon/I-80 (Parleys Summit) + East Canyon Road, 38 miles
- Draper Loop + Camp Williams Loop, 38 miles
- Traverse Mountain Loop + Draper-Herriman Loop, 40 miles
- Traverse Mountain Loop + Camp Williams Loop + Draper Loop, 40 miles
- Josie Johnson + Wasatch Boulevard + Dimple Dell Loop (Draper), 42 miles
- Bountiful Bench + North Salt Lake Loop, 47 miles
- Traverse Mountains Loop + Camp Williams Loop + Draper-Herriman Loop, 48 miles
- Traverse Mountains Loop + Camp Williams Loop + Draper-Herriman Loop + West Jordan–Bluffdale Loop, 63 miles

- Josie Johnson + Wasatch Boulevard + Dimple Dell Loop (Draper) + Traverse Mountains Loop, 66 miles
- Josie Johnson + Wasatch Boulevard + Dimple Dell Loop (Draper) + Draper-Herriman Loop, 67 miles
- Josie Johnson + Wasatch Boulevard + Dimple Dell Loop (Draper) + Traverse Mountains Loop + Camp Williams Loop + Draper-Herriman Loop, 89 miles
- Josie Johnson + Wasatch Boulevard + Dimple Dell Loop (Draper) + Traverse Mountains Loop + Camp Williams Loop + Draper-Herriman Loop + West Jordan–BluffdaleLoop, 104 miles

Mountain
Biking
Rides

1 Bonneville Shoreline Trail (Ensign Peak)

Riding along a shoreline should be flat and easy, right? Not when you're pursuing the Ensign Peak section of the Bonneville Shoreline Trail (BST), because getting to the actual bench requires strong legs and ultra-low gears. Reward for your effort, however, is a staggering view of the entire Salt Lake Valley, from the State Capitol to Point of the Mountain, and of the lofty Wasatch Range and Oquirrh Mountains that enclose the valley. Along with the climbs, there are some fast, smooth sections, too.

Start: City Creek Canyon Trailhead.

Distance: 11.2-mile out-and-back.

Gain: 1,500 feet.

Physical difficulty: Moderately strenuous. Although not a long ride, there are two burly climbs. First is the low-gear grunt from City Creek Canyon to the Ensign Peak ridge on the way out, then the steady grind out of Jones Canyon on the way back.

Technical difficulty: 2 to 4. The switchbacks rising out of City Creek Canyon are steep, sharp, and difficult to ride up; they're tricky on the descent, too. The climb out of Jones Canyon follows a rocky doubletrack. The rest of the route is smooth-rolling doubletracks and singletracks.

Trail surface: 6.4 miles on singletrack; 4.8 miles on doubletrack.

Season: March through June and September through November. Midday during midsummer is deathly hot when temperatures near 100 degrees.

Land status: USFS Salt Lake Ranger District, Salt Lake City, and North Salt Lake City.

Maps: USGS 1:24,000: Fort Douglas and Salt Lake City North, Utah.

Finding the trailhead: From anywhere in Salt Lake, make your way through the Avenues to the intersection of B Street and 11th Avenue. Take Bonneville Boulevard 0.7 mile to City Creek Canyon Road. (Bonneville Boulevard is one-way for vehicles, east to west. It's two-way for bikes and pedestrians.) Park at the BST lot (limited space) or just up City Creek Canyon Road (also limited space). This trail begins on the west side of the intersection.

Know before you go: The BST is open to bikes every day; however, bicycles are allowed on the City Creek Canyon Road on odd-numbered calendar days only. Except for on the BST, bicycles are prohibited off-road in City Creek Canyon. Rattlesnakes are known to inhabit these warm foothills.

The Ride

0.0 From the trailhead at the intersection of Bonneville Boulevard and City Creek Canyon Road, chug up the dirt and gravel path on the old cross-country ski trail. The path rises moderately through brushy oak and maple, but there are a few short, steep climbs thrown in for good measure. The paved City Creek Canyon Road is right beneath you.

1.0 Fork left on the BST to begin the arduous climb out of the canyon. Bikes are prohibited on the ski trail past the BST junction. You know you're on the right route when you face half a dozen steep, tight switchbacks that are difficult to negotiate without teetering.

1.5 Pass beneath ruddy cliffs of chunky conglomerate and high above ritzy homes in the exclusive Eagle Gate community.

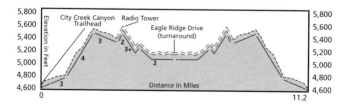

Bonneville Shoreline Trail (Ensign Peak)

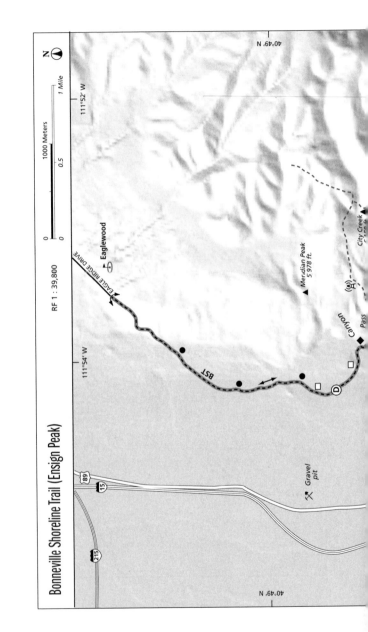

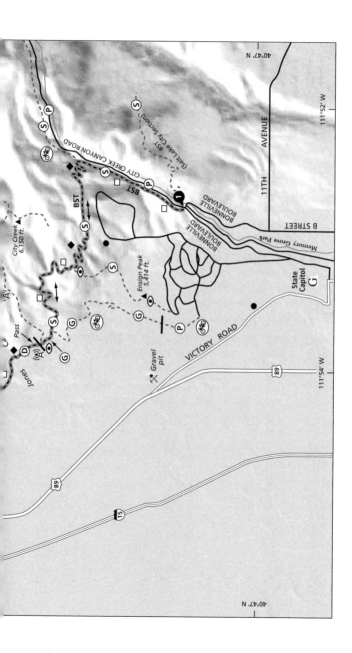

Gear down (if you have any gears left, that is) and attack more steep, tight switchbacks.

2.1 Reach the ridge that extends left/south to Ensign Peak. The BST forks right on the ridge, then immediately left, and contours across the sunny, brushy hillsides. You'll freewheel generously, but on the return you'll pedal continuously. **Side-trip:** For a colossal view of the Salt Lake Valley, turn left at the ridge toward Ensign Peak.

3.1 Intersect a gravel service road, and take it right and uphill.

3.3 Come to a pass next to a communication tower. Go straight over the pass and descend the rock-pocked doubletrack around a gate. This will be the toughest climb on the return leg.

3.5 Bend through Jones Canyon, bottom out, and climb quickly; then descend like wind-fanned wildfire to a broad, grassy bench that is the wave-cut shoreline of ancient Lake Bonneville. Cruise easily on the level, smooth doubletrack.

5.6 Come to Eagle Ridge Drive, and turn around. (Note: Obey signs limiting access through the residential area.)

11.2 Arrive back at the City Creek Canyon Trailhead.

2 Bonneville Shoreline Trail (Salt Lake City)

The cornerstone of the entire 250-mile proposed Bonneville Shoreline Trail (BST), the Salt Lake City section combines challenging climbs and exciting descents to and from the smooth-rolling "shoreline" of ancient Lake Bonneville. Views of the Salt Lake metro area, as it laps against the lofty Wasatch Range, are postcard perfect. Two tough climbs (up Dry Creek and up from the City Creek Canyon Trailhead) might make the whole route beyond the reach of novices, but multiple trailheads offer countless short courses that cater to everyone.

Start: Sunnyside Avenue Trailhead at mouth of Emigration Canyon.

Distance: 10-mile one-way with a shuttle.

Gain: 1,300 feet from Emigration Canyon to City Creek Canyon, or 1,600 feet from City Creek Canyon to Emigration Canyon.

Physical difficulty: Moderate, one-way; strenuous, round-trip. There are several difficult climbs in between the otherwise level "shoreline." Most notable are the mile-long climb up Dry Creek and the short stinging grunt past Twin Peaks (when riding east to west), and the continual grind from City Creek Canyon to the Bobsled saddle (when riding west to east). If you ride out-and-back (20 miles), you're in for a solid workout, but shorter flights from selected trailheads can be moderately easy.

Technical difficulty: 2 to 3+. The BST packs lots of smooth-running trail, but there are many choppy sections that may force novice riders to dismount briefly. Some climbs, although mostly smooth, are steep and require raw power and good slow-speed balance.

Trail surface: 6.5 miles on single-track; 3.5 miles on doubletrack.
Season: March through June and September through November. Midday during midsummer is deathly hot when temperatures near 100 degrees.

Land status: USFS Salt Lake Ranger District, Salt Lake City Municipal, and University of Utah.
Maps: USGS 1:24,000: Fort Douglas, Utah.

Finding the trailhead: Sunnyside Avenue Trailhead: From the intersection of Foothill Drive (1950 East) and Sunnyside Avenue (850 South), take Sunnyside 1 mile east to the trailhead parking lot at the mouth of Emigration Canyon, opposite Crestview Drive and Hogle Zoo. City Creek Canyon Trailhead: From the intersection of Sunnyside Avenue and Foothill Drive, take Foothill north then west (becomes 500 South). Turn right/north on 1300 East, go right on South Temple Street, and turn left on Virginia Street (1345 East). Turn left/west on 11th Avenue opposite Popperton Park (trailhead for Dry Creek access). Take 11th Avenue to the intersection with B Street, and go right on Bonneville Boulevard (one-way east to west for vehicles) to the City Creek Canyon Trailhead.

The BST can be accessed from other trailheads as well. Red Butte Canyon: From Foothill Drive on the southeast side of the University of Utah, take Wasatch Drive and turn right on Hempstead. Travel east through Fort Douglas and park at the lot for Red Butte Gardens and Arboretum. Terrace Hills Drive: From 11th Avenue at about 1000 East (opposite the fire station), turn north on Terrace Hills Drive and park after 0.8 mile at the end of the street. Please respect private residences. Morris Reservoir: From 11th Avenue go up I Street, fork left on Northhills Drive, and curve right on 18th Avenue. The parking area is next to the Church of Jesus Christ of Latter-day Saints.

Know before you go: The BST is very popular with pedestrians as well as mountain bikers, so yield the trail, control your speed, and anticipate other trail users. Navigation can be challenging because the BST passes junctions with many side trails; however, the BST is adequately signed. You can't get "lost," only perhaps confused. Rattlesnakes are known to inhabit these warm foothills. Bikes are not allowed on dirt roads or trails within This is the Place State Park.

The Ride

Here's the ride going east to west, from Sunnyside Avenue (Emigration Canyon) to City Creek Canyon. Note that the ride is equally popular ridden west to east.

If you are riding from City Creek Canyon to Emigration Canyon, prepare yourself for 3 miles of steep intermittent climbs to the pipeline saddle above the Bobsled. The rest of the BST is gravy.

0.0 Start at the Sunnyside Avenue Trailhead at the mouth of Emigration Canyon. Squeeze through the fence gap and gear down for a short, stiff climb. Stay left alongside the log fence, then veer right onto a doubletrack heading uphill.

0.4 Go left at a T-junction with a dirt road, and descend past a trail forking right and uphill.

0.5 Turn right onto the signed BST singletrack (if you miss the turn, you'll enter This is the Place State Park, where bikes are prohibited) and roll uphill gradually, passing more trails forking right.

1.0 Top out on a pipeline corridor (doubletrack) and squeeze through a gap in the chain-link fence. Take the left-hand lane (doubletrack) overlooking Research Park and all of the Salt Lake Valley.

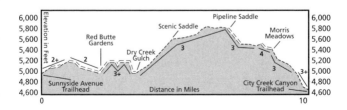

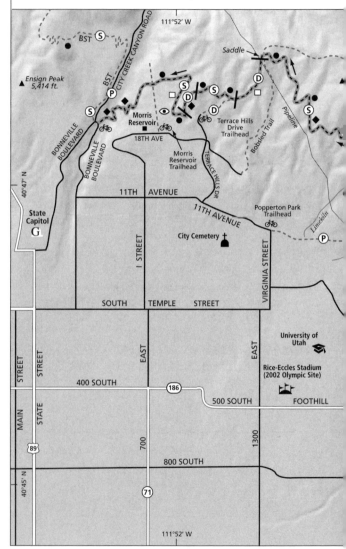

Bonneville Shoreline Trail (Salt Lake City)

BST S

BST

CITY CREEK CANYON ROAD

111°52' W

Saddle

Ensign Peak
5,414 ft.

P

S

S

D

D

D

Morris
Reservoir

18TH AVE

Morris
Reservoir
Trailhead

Terrace Hills
Drive
Trailhead

Bobsled Trail

Pipeline

S

BONNEVILLE BOULEVARD

BONNEVILLE BOULEVARD

TERRACE HILLS DR

40°47' N

11TH AVENUE

11TH AVENUE

Popperton Park
Trailhead

Lincoln

State
Capitol
G

I STREET

City Cemetery

VIRGINIA STREET

P

SOUTH TEMPLE STREET

STREET

STREET

MAIN

STATE

EAST

EAST

University of
Utah

Rice-Eccles Stadium
(2002 Olympic Site)

FOOTHILL

400 SOUTH

186

500 SOUTH

89

700

1300

800 SOUTH

71

40°45' N

111°52' W

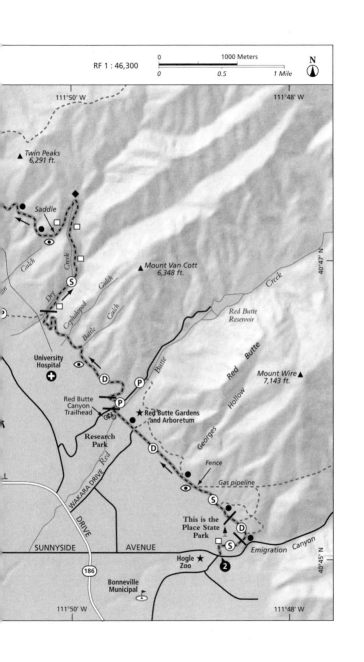

RF 1 : 46,300

0   1000 Meters
0   0.5   1 Mile

N

111°50' W

111°48' W

▲ Twin Peaks
6,291 ft.

Saddle

▲ Mount Van Cott
6,348 ft.

40°47' N

Red Butte
Reservoir

Creek

Gulch

Dry

Creek

Cephalopod

Battle

Gulch

Gulch

Red

Butte

University
Hospital

▲ Mount Wire
7,143 ft.

D

P

P

Red Butte
Canyon Trailhead

★ Red Butte Gardens
and Arboretum

Butte

Hollow

Georges

Research
Park

WAKARA DRIVE

Red

D

Fence

Gas pipeline

S

This is the
Place State
Park

D

40°45' N

SUNNYSIDE   AVENUE

S

Emigration Canyon

186

Hogle ★
Zoo

2

Bonneville
Municipal

DRIVE

111°50' W

111°48' W

2.0 After crossing the paved entrance road to Red Butte Gardens and Arboretum, cross over Red Butte Creek and come to Red Butte Canyon Road (north entrance to the arboretum and alternate trailhead). Go right up the paved Red Butte Canyon Road 0.1 mile, fork left on a paved lane, and then turn right immediately onto a gravel doubletrack (might not be signed). Climb steeply to the power line doubletrack on the shoreline bench. More panoramic views! Cross two gulches: the first is a quick, technical drop and climb; the second is a contour on very narrow trail. The University of Utah Health Sciences Center is below the trail.

3.1 Angle left and downhill off the shoreline. Go right on a dirt road to the mouth of Dry Creek Gulch. (The Popperton Park/11th Avenue Trailhead is to the left along the paved path.)

3.5 Enter Dry Creek Gulch. Gear down and climb moderately up the, uh, dry creek.

4.5 Switchback left and pump at full force out of the gulch.

4.8 Top out at a scenic saddle above Limekiln Gulch. The old lime kilns can be seen below the trail. Traverse the sunny foothills above the Avenues.

5.8 Bend right and gear down for the short, steep grunt past Twin Peaks on your right, a.k.a. "Ring Hill," where the five rings of the 2002 Winter Olympic Games shined brightly. Enjoy a long, smooth, rolling traverse with stunning views of Salt Lake City backed by the Wasatch Range.

7.0 Come to a multiple junction in a saddle through which a buried pipeline crosses. Take the doubletrack veering left and descending gradually. (Don't take the first left, which drops steeply along the pipeline corridor, unless you want to pursue the infamous Bobsled Trail.)

7.5 Where the power lines are overhead, fork right onto the continued BST singletrack. (The doubletrack continues downhill to the Terrace Hills Drive Trailhead.) Weave through the hollows and connect with a pebbly doubletrack on a knoll and descend sharply to a water tank.

8.3 Fork right at the water tank, traverse above the Utah State Capitol, and glide down to and across Morris Meadows.

9.0 Go straight at a four-way junction of trails in Morris Meadows (left leads to the Morris Reservoir/18th Avenue Trailhead, and right is a dead end). A switchbacking descent on narrow trail drops to the City Creek Canyon Trailhead. Control your speed and be courteous to other trail users.

10.0 Arrive at City Creek Canyon Trailhead on Bonneville Boulevard.

3 Mormon Pioneer Trail

One of Salt Lake's newest trails, the Mormon Pioneer Trail is quickly becoming one of the area's most popular. Following the route of the Mormon Pioneers of 1847, the path rises up Mountain Dell Canyon to Big Mountain Pass, where vistas of the Wasatch Range and the distant Salt Lake Valley inspired the Church of Jesus Christ of Latter-day Saints leader Brigham Young to declare, "This is the Place." The lower trail from the highway trailhead to Affleck Park is moderately pitched and thus caters to novice riders. The upper section rises steeply with periodic rough tread and tight turns and is reserved for intermediate mountain bikers or stronger.

Start: Trailhead on Highway 65, 10.5 miles east of Salt Lake City.
Distance: 6.8-mile out-and-back.
Gain: 1,420 feet.

Physical difficulty: Moderately strenuous. From the trailhead to Affleck Park is moderately easy with gentle grades; from Affleck Park to Big Mountain Pass is strenuous with steep climbs and sharp switchbacks.

Technical difficulty: 2 to 4. There is smooth, hard-packed dirt from the trailhead to Affleck Park, and hard-packed dirt with loose choppy tread on the steeper stuff from Affleck to the summit (may require periodic dismounts and brief walking). The downhill ride is a blast.

Trail surface: All singletrack.

Season: May through October.

Land status: USFS Salt Lake Ranger District and Salt Lake City Watershed Management.

Maps: USGS 1:24,000: Mountain Dell, Utah.

Finding the trailhead: From Salt Lake City take Interstate 80 east into Parleys Canyon. Drive 6 miles up I–80 and take exit 134 for East Canyon and Mountain Dell. Drive north on Highway 65 for 4.6 miles to the highway trailhead, passing the turnoff for Emigration Canyon and the entrance to Little Dell Reservoir Recreation Area along the way.

Know before you go: Dogs are not allowed because the trail is within the Mountain Dell Watershed. The trail is popular with hikers, so ride courteously and cautiously, especially when descending. Affleck Park and Little Dell Reservoir Recreation Area are fee areas, but there is no fee to park at the highway trailhead. There is an outhouse at the highway trailhead, at Affleck Park, and at Big Mountain Pass, but there are no water taps.

The Ride

0.0 From the highway trailhead cross the road to the west side and pick up the signed trail near a steel gate. Gear down for

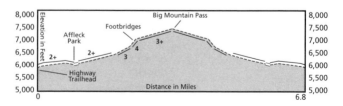

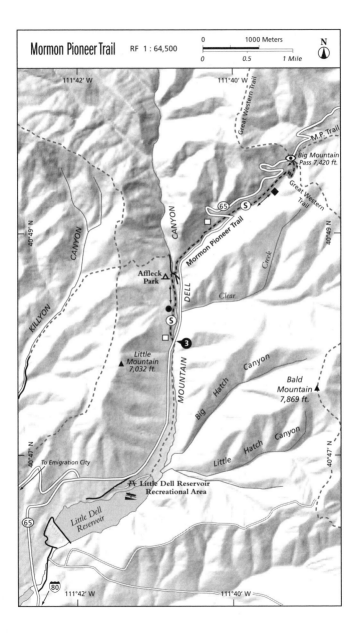

Mormon Pioneer Trail

RF 1 : 64,500

0   1000 Meters

0   0.5   1 Mile

N

111°42' W

111°40' W

Great Western Trail

M.P. Trail

Big Mountain Pass 7,420 ft.

65

S

Mormon Pioneer Trail

Great Western Trail

40°49' N

40°49' N

CANYON

DELL

Clear

Creek

Affleck Park

S

3

MOUNTAIN

Little Mountain 7,032 ft.

KILLYON

CANYON

Big Hatch Canyon

Bald Mountain 7,869 ft.

40°47' N

Little Hatch Canyon

40°47' N

To Emigration City

Little Dell Reservoir Recreational Area

65

Little Dell Reservoir

80

111°42' W

111°40' W

a short, steep climb, then relax and spin up the sunny trail. Big Mountain Pass hides just out of sight beyond the rocky cliffs and timbered slopes of upper Mountain Dell Canyon.

0.8   Enter Affleck Park. Go left on the dirt road, then fork right immediately on a dirt road and cross the bridge over the creek. Now go left through the large dirt parking area and pass the interpretive signs that describe the Mormon Pioneers' 1847 trek.

0.9   Pick up the continued trail at the end of the park's dirt road. The smooth trail rises moderately across small meadows and through patches of shadowy oak, maple, and conifers. You'll have to pump hard briefly up a few tiny hills.

1.9   Round two sharp turns and cross the highway, cautiously! Gear down. The trail angles up more steeply and the tread is pebbly. Climb steadily, then take some deep breaths and power up a sharp, eroded hill.

2.4   Cross two footbridges and teeter around the first of half a dozen switchbacks. In between the turns you'll enjoy smooth, gradually rising trail tucked in the trees.

3.4   A long ascending traverse through aspens takes you to the parking area at Big Mountain Pass. Here the 3,000-mile-long Great Western Trail crosses the pass on its way from Canada to Mexico. Read the interpretive signs about the Mormons' passing and enjoy the vista beyond Mountain Dell Canyon to the Mill Creek Canyon ridge and to the Salt Lake Valley. You can even make out Kennecott's Bingham Canyon Copper Mine on the faraway Oquirrh Mountains. Enjoy freewheeling all the way back to the trailhead; you deserve it. Control your speed because sections of the trail have limited sight lines and other recreationists might be present. Watch out for those footbridges; they come up fast, and loose dirt on their surfaces can be slippery.

6.8   Arrive back at the trailhead.

4 Mill Creek Pipeline Trail

If you want to experience the joy of riding on singletrack, but don't want to scale entire mountains to do so, then you should try Mill Creek Pipeline Trail. The path follows an old water flume on the flank of Mill Creek Canyon where the bulk of the ride descends at nearly imperceptible grades. Three quick, rough descents, however, make the ride exciting for even veteran mountain bikers. You'll ride through tunnels of oak, maple, and pine and then cross treeless slopes that afford inspiring views of the canyon's depths and of peaks in the Mount Olympus Wilderness. With four trailheads on the paved Mill Creek Canyon Road, the Pipeline Trail can be ridden as loops of varying difficulty as well.

Start: Elbow Fork trailhead on Mill Creek Canyon Road.
Distance: 7.2-mile one-way with a shuttle.
Gain: 150 feet; 1,450-foot loss.
Physical difficulty: Moderately easy. Most of the trail is nearly flat, but there are three short, challenging descents that can unnerve a rank beginner. If you're not ashamed to walk the rough stuff, then you'll find the rest of the trail to be dreamy. Converting the ride to a loop makes it moderately strenuous.
Technical difficulty: 2 to 4+. There is lots of flat, smooth-

rolling tread but three short, steep, rough, switchbacking descents. Ride what you can and walk the rest.
Trail surface: All singletrack. The loop options require use of paved road.
Season: April through June and September through October. Midday during midsummer is very hot; start early!
Land status: USFS Salt Lake Ranger District.
Maps: USGS 1:24,000: Mount Aire and Sugarhouse, Utah.

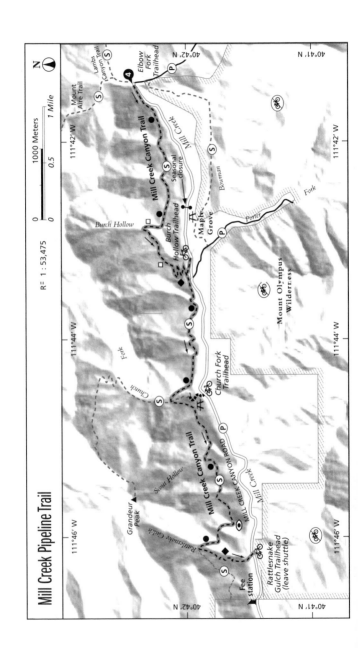

Mill Creek Pipeline Trail

R= 1 : 53,475

quickly and ask that you review your purchase below.

M3A-570509

4BQG5300C87H

Title	BICYCLING SALT LAKE CITY: A GUID
Condition	Very Good
Location	Aisle 63 Section 9 Shelf 8 Item 432
Description	A well-cared-for item that has seen limited use but remains in great condition. The item is complete, unmarked, and undamaged, but may show some limited signs of wear. Item works perfectly. Pages are intact and not marred by notes or highlighting. The spine is undamaged.
ASIN	0762740965
Employee	1876

If anything is incorrect, please contact us immediately at orders@jensononline.com and we will make it right. Thank you again for your purchase and please leave feedback online!

Finding the trailhead: If traveling south on Interstate 215 from Interstate 80, take exit 4 (3900 South) and go left to the intersection of 3900 South and Wasatch Boulevard. If traveling north on I-215, take exit 4 (3900 South/3300 South) and go straight to the intersection of 3900 South and Wasatch Boulevard. In both cases, drive 1 block north on Wasatch Boulevard to 3800 South and turn right/east on Mill Creek Canyon Road. The fee station is in 0.7 mile. Rattlesnake Gulch is 0.7 mile past the fee station. Leave one vehicle here and shuttle 4.7 miles up Mill Creek Canyon Road to the Elbow Fork Trailhead.

Know before you go: Mill Creek Canyon is a fee area: $2.25 per vehicle, payable upon leaving the canyon. There is no fee for bicyclists pedaling up the road through the fee station. Dogs must be leashed on this trail on even-numbered calendar days. Mill Creek Canyon Road is closed to vehicles above Maple Grove Picnic Area from November 1 to June 30, so during this time of year you must pedal up the road from Maple Grove to the Elbow Fork Trailhead. Pipeline Trail is popular with hikers and runners, so ride attentively and courteously. This is not a race course! The trail is a scorcher at midday during midsummer. Consequently, it's a good early- and late-season choice.

The Ride

0.0 From the Elbow Fork Trailhead, be sure to take the Pipeline Trail (flat) into the trees and not the combined Mount Aire/Lambs Canyon Trail (steep) next to the outhouse. Suddenly, the canyon drops below your left pedal and rock walls

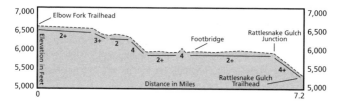

brush by your right shoulder. Eyes forward; don't look down! Some choppy rocks in the tread can bounce you around. Keep on the straight and narrow because you don't want to get bounced around too much here. In short order the trail smooths and is more forgiving.

1.4 Stay straight where the Burch Hollow Trail forks right and rises uphill steeply.

1.6 The trail bends sharply right and affords a view of Mount Raymond and Gobblers Knob across the canyon. Hunker down for a short, steep, rutted descent into Burch Hollow proper, then relish smooth-running trail enveloped by trees.

2.3 Begin the choppy switchbacking descent to the Burch Hollow Trailhead. Beginners might want to walk parts. There is a good view of Porter Fork dropping from Mount Raymond across the canyon.

2.7 At a T-junction go right to continue on the Pipeline Trail; otherwise go left 100 yards to the Burch Hollow Trailhead on Mill Creek Canyon Road. Continuing, you'll enjoy easy cruising as the trail contours through timber and across open slopes.

3.0 Aromas from Log Haven Restaurant, just below the trail, waft through the timber. Alas, you have your tasty energy bar to choke down.

3.9 A small cliff brushes by your right shoulder, signaling you to gear down quickly and pump hard up "sucker hill." If you're caught in the wrong gear, then you'll understand. Hold on tight for a quick little drop on rough tread next to a wood-plank retaining wall that keeps the trail from falling off the hillside.

4.3 Intersect Grandeur Peak Trail and cross a footbridge over Church Fork creek. Go straight to continue on Pipeline Trail, or fork left to descend steeply on the dirt trail, then on a paved lane, to Mill Creek Canyon Road about half a mile away. Pipeline Trail contours again into timbered hollows and out across sunny treeless slopes. Mount Olympus comes into view across the canyon, and a wedge of the Salt Lake Valley can be seen in the distance through the canyon's entrance.

6.4 Intersect Rattlesnake Gulch Trail. Fork left for the wickedly steep, rutted, rocky descent to the Rattlesnake Gulch Trailhead. Ride what you can and walk the rest. Switchbacks are supertight, and gravel in the lower gulch rolls beneath your tires like ball bearings. **Option:** You can tack on about 1.2 miles more, out-and-back, by going past the Rattlesnake Gulch Trail junction on the continued Pipeline Trail. Obey travel restrictions where the trail leaves the national forest and enters private land.

7.2 Arrive at the Rattlesnake Gulch Trailhead. What an ending. How about riding in reverse and climbing Rattlesnake Gulch next time? Ugh!

5 Big Water Trail

Inquire locally about the best intermediate-level mountain bike ride in Salt Lake, and the Big Water Trail to Dog Lake will be the unchallenged response. Newbies, veterans, locals, and visitors alike will rave about Big Water's smooth-rolling tread and evenly pitched grade. The alpine pond at the trail's end is perfect for wallowing away the afternoon under a shady tree or basking in the warm midday sun. You won't find jaw-dropping vistas of jagged peaks or glacially carved canyons on Big Water because the trail is tightly embraced by pristine aspens and conifers underlain by thick brush and showy wildflowers. It's a short ride, but it's so sweet.

Start: Big Water trailhead, 9.7 miles up Mill Creek Canyon.
Distance: 6.4-mile out-and-back.
Gain: 1,200 feet.
Physical difficulty: Moderate. If you're a novice rider, you might find the steady climb taxing, but don't be deterred because there are boatloads of buffed trail, and the return descent is one of the sweetest in the Wasatch. Some choppy stretches, root hops, and

frequent switchbacks keep the ride upbeat for stronger riders.
Technical difficulty: 2 to 3+. Buffed trail abounds, but you'll have opportunities to perfect your root-hopping and switchback-rounding skills, too.
Trail surface: All singletrack.
Season: Mid-May through October.
Land status: USFS Salt Lake Ranger District.
Maps: USGS 1:24,000: Mount Aire, Utah.

Finding the trailhead: If traveling south on Interstate 215, take exit 4 (3900 South), turn left on 3900 South, and go to the intersection with Wasatch Boulevard. If traveling north on I-215, take exit 4 (3900 South/3300 South) and go to the intersection of 3900 South and Wasatch Boulevard. In both cases, drive 1 block north to 3800 South and turn right/east on Mill Creek Canyon Road. The fee station is in 0.7 mile. Drive 9 miles past the fee station to where the road ends at the double parking lots.

Know before you go: Big Water Trail is perhaps the most popular trail in the Wasatch Range, so rest assured you'll encounter mountain bikers, hikers, and occasionally equestrians. Ride at prudent speeds, especially when descending, and yield to other trail users. Parking lots fill up quickly on weekends, so you may have to park below the trailhead and bike a short ways up the road. There is an outhouse at the trailhead but no water tap.

Bikes are allowed on Upper Mill Creek Canyon trails (Big Water Trail, Little Water Trail, and Great Western Trail) on *even-numbered* calendar days from July 1 to October 31. Bikes are allowed every day from November 1 to June 30, but the trail might be closed because of snow. Dogs must be leashed on these same trails on *even-numbered* calendar days, so riding with your pet has become all but obsolete. Mill Creek Canyon Road is closed to vehicles above Maple Grove Picnic Area from November 1 to June 30 (4 miles up from the fee station and 4.5 miles below the Big Water Trailhead). If the trail is snow free during this time, you must pedal 4.5 miles up the road first.

Mill Creek Canyon is a fee area. Vehicles are charged $2.25 upon exiting the canyon. Bicycles and pedestrians are not charged the fee.

The Ride

0.0 Start at the Lower Big Water Trail parking lot. Gear down because the first quarter mile is one of the trail's steepest

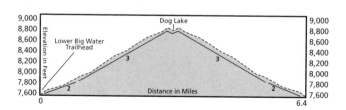

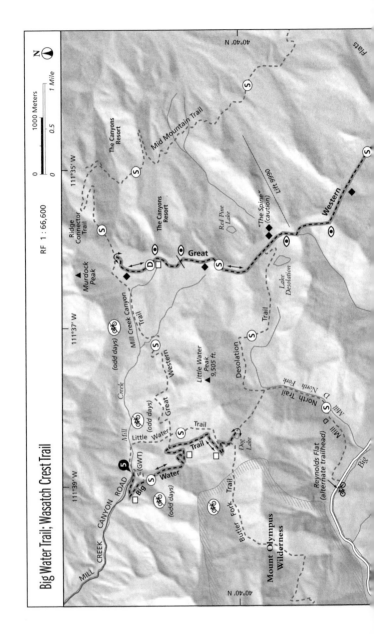

Big Water Trail; Wasatch Crest Trail

RF 1 : 66,600

N

0   1000 Meters
0   0.5   1 Mile

111°39' W   111°37' W   111°35' W

40°40' N

MILL CREEK CANYON ROAD

Mill Creek

Murdock Peak

Ridge Connector Trail

The Canyons Resort

Mid Mountain Trail

Mill Creek Canyon Trail

Western

Little Water Peak 9,505 ft.

Great

Little Water (GWT)

Big Water

Great

Western

Trail

Trail

Dog Lake

Butler Fork Trail

Mount Olympus Wilderness

Reynolds Flat (alternate trailhead)

North Fork

North Trail

Mill

Mill

Desolation Trail

Red Pine Lake

Lake Desolation

"The Spine" (caution)

Lift 9990

Great

Western

Flats

Big

(odd days)

(odd days)

(odd days)

(odd days)

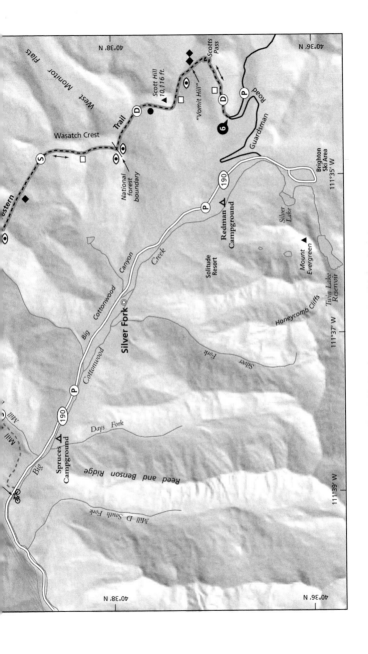

parts, but it's no match for a mountain bike's ultra-low gears. Teeter around a left turn and chug up through stately conifers on baby-butt-smooth trail. Who needs full-suspension?

0.5 The Great Western Trail (GWT) intersects from the left and both trails become one.

1.0 Cross the footbridge over Big Water Creek on a left bend and climb across aspen slopes. Reenter the darkened conifers and climb two switchbacks. Cross a narrow footbridge over a tributary and climb again through aspens.

1.5 Bend right near two small knolls (a good rest stop) and go straight where the GWT forks left into upper Mill Creek Canyon and toward Wasatch Crest. Climb steadily on tight, smooth tread with periodic chop and roots.

2.4 Cross Little Water Trail, then round a sharp right turn. You can climb Little Water to the top, but it's a bit steeper. You can descend Little Water Trail to the trailhead, but it's definitely steeper and more technical than Big Water.

3.1 Little Water Trail joins Big Water from the right. Arrive at a junction signed for Mount Olympus Wilderness (right), Dog Lake (left), and Lake Desolation (left). Go left and down the short gravelly hill to Dog Lake on what is officially the Desolation Trail.

3.2 At Dog Lake enjoy snacks, sun, and a snooze; then retrace your tracks.

6.4 Arrive back at the parking lot.

6 Wasatch Crest Trail

Undoubtedly the premier mountain bike trail in northern Utah, the Wasatch Crest Trail follows the "Backbone of Utah" and is a must-ride for anyone new to this neck of the woods. At nearly 10,000 feet in elevation, this ridgetop singletrack requires pistons for legs and bellows for lungs, but it serves up sweet singletrack through pristine aspens and across wildflower-dotted alpine bowls. Pack along your camera because the glacial-carved peaks and canyons, wildflower slopes, and dense aspen groves of the Wasatch are postcard perfect. Best of all, many options exist by which to shorten, extend, or make loops out of the standard out–and–back ride.

See map on pages 38–39.

Start: Guardsman Road trailhead at the top of Big Cottonwood Canyon.

Distance: 15.2-mile out-and-back.

Gain: 2,600 feet for the entire out-and-back route.

Physical difficulty: Strenuous for the entire route. Shorter options are still strenuous because everyone, regardless of their destination, has to endure "Vomit Hill" early in the ride. The Wasatch Crest Trail proper undulates along the ridgetop with fast, gradual descents and moderate climbs. Remember, downhills that make you scream with glee on the way out will make you sweat like a dog on the way back.

Technical difficulty: 2+ to 5. Tight, smooth-rolling singletrack highlights the Crest Trail (tech 3), but there are choppy and washboarded stretches, too (tech 4). "The Spine" is a 100-yard hike-a-bike over jagged bedrock (tech 5). Doubletrack sections vary from hard-packed dirt (tech 2+) to choppy, loose gravel (tech 3+).

Trail surface: 9.2 miles on singletrack and 6 miles on doubletrack for the entire out-and-back ride.

Season: Late June through October.

Land status: USFS Salt Lake Ranger District.

Maps: USGS 1:24,000: Brighton, Mount Aire, and Park City West, Utah.

Finding the trailhead: From Interstate 215 take exit 6 (6200 South, Ski Areas) and travel east on 6200 South, then south on Wasatch Boulevard to 7200 South/Fort Union Boulevard. Take Big Cottonwood Canyon Road/Highway 190 for 14 miles and fork left on Guardsman Road (1.3 miles past Solitude and 0.5 mile before Brighton). Park along the road's edge 2 miles up Guardsman Road on the second right-hand switchback. Take the dirt road down to the red gate, lift your bike over, and you're off. Do not block the dirt road or gate.

Know before you go: Be prepared for rapidly changing alpine weather. The Wasatch Crest is very popular, so expect and respect other users. If your destination is Mill Creek Canyon, then remember that bikes are allowed on upper Mill Creek Canyon trails on even-numbered calendar days only from July 1 to November 1. Bikes are not allowed on odd-numbered calendar days. Dogs (and horses) are not allowed in the Big Cottonwood Canyon Watershed.

The Ride

0.0 From the Guardsman Road Trailhead, go down the dirt road and lift your bike over the big steel gate, then chug up through shadowy fir trees on doubletrack.

0.7 Pump hard up a short, steep hill to Scotts Pass. Park City Mountain Resort lies on the other side of the pass. Fork left on a doubletrack, climb past a steel gate, and curve around two switchbacks. Breathe deeply, settle into your granny gear, and prepare to do battle with the infamous "Vomit Hill." The hill's steep grade and pebbly doubletrack are sinister. You might feel like you'll blow up (or blow chunks) by the time you reach the top.

1.2 At the top of Vomit Hill, collect yourself and then follow the doubletrack westward. Check out the view of upper Big Cottonwood Canyon. Solitude and Brighton ski areas are at your feet, and you are eye-to-eye with the resorts' rough-cut peaks. Curve past the communication towers, cross the top of U.S.A. Bowl (a backcountry skiers' haunt), then zoom past Scott Hill (more communication towers).

2.6 Doubletrack narrows to singletrack as the route crosses into the Wasatch National Forest. This is another stellar viewpoint. Tight singletrack rolls across the tops of alpine bowls and slips through stands of crookneck aspens. Sweet! Keep your front wheel on the straight and narrow, or you risk taking a big tumble. Gear down for a half-mile climb to another viewpoint. Mount Raymond and Gobblers Knob are to the west.

5.1 Photo op! The trail traverses high above Lake Desolation. Dismount for the hike-a-bike down "the Spine." Glaciers once gnawed at the ridge, leaving behind jags of red-brown and maroon quartzite that are virtually impossible to ride over. This is a good turnaround point because if you pursue the rest of the ride, you'll just have to hoof it up the Spine on the return.

5.3 Fork right at the junction with Desolation Trail and climb gradually through an aspen glade to the Big Cottonwood Canyon Watershed boundary. Roll along the forested ridge on smooth and bouldery singletrack.

6.3 Drop down a rough hill, which is another hike-a-bike on the return leg, and pass a viewpoint of The Canyons Resort. Singletrack reverts to doubletrack, which rides like singletrack

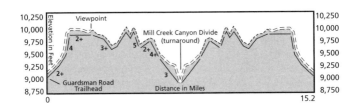

anyway. Pass a second viewpoint of The Canyons and descend rapidly on choppy tread through aspens and firs.

7.6 Enter a meadow at the Mill Creek Canyon Divide. Turn around and retrace your tracks. Hope you're packing lots of energy because there are many hills to climb.

15.2 Arrive back at the trailhead.

7 Solitude Mountain Resort

Downhill cruising is the fare at Solitude, but you won't find gangs of armor-clad warriors bombing the trails either. Solitude's compact trail system is cross-country-style in nature, combining long descending traverses and well-carved switchbacks. Although gravity rules once you step off Sunrise Lift, there is plenty of climbing available if you start from the base or use Sunrise as a stepping-stone for ascents to Solitude's highest points. The Intermountain Cup Mountain Bike Race Series stops at Solitude annually, and racers continually rave about the course's challenging climbs and blazing descents.

But wait, there's more: mountain scooters, disc golf, hiking, and fishing. When you're through with your outdoor adventure, you can kick back at the Village and listen to live music, catch a snack on the deck, or dine at one of the resort's fine restaurants.

Start: Solitude Mountain Resort, 13 miles up Big Cottonwood Canyon.

Distance: Varies; there are about 13.5 miles of mountain biking routes.

Loss: 800 feet from the top of Sunrise Lift to the base. If you like to climb, however, you can easily rack up a couple thousand feet.

Physical difficulty: Moderately easy to extremely strenuous.

Gravity is your friend as you exit the top of Sunrise Lift, but short climbs on some trails will jump-start your heart. If you snub the lift ride and climb from the base, then difficulty ranges from moderately strenuous on the main service road to extremely strenuous if you ride to the top of either Powderhorn or Summit Lifts.

Technical difficulty: 2 to 4+. The trail system is a combination of buffed singletrack and hard-packed dirt roads with sections of loose and rocky tread, ruts, and washboards.

Trail surface: 5.7 miles of singletrack; 7.8 miles of doubletrack.

Season: June through September, weather permitting.

Land status: USFS Salt Lake Ranger District and Solitude Mountain Resort.

Maps: USGS 1:24,000: Brighton, Utah. Trail map is available at Solitude or www.skisolitude.com.

Finding the trailhead: From Interstate 215 take exit 6 (6200 South, Ski Areas). Travel east on 6200 South, then south on Wasatch Boulevard to 7200 South/Fort Union Boulevard. Travel 12.8 miles up Big Cottonwood Canyon on Highway 190 to entry 2 for Solitude Mountain Resort (Village at Solitude).

Know before you go: Sunrise Lift operates Thursday and Friday from 1:00 to 6:00 P.M. and Saturday and Sunday from 10:00 A.M. to 6:00 P.M. Lift rates are $6 for a single ride and $24 for all day. Children under six ride for free. Trails are open for use every day, and there is no trail-use fee if you choose not to ride the lift. Bike rentals, accessories, drinks, and snacks are available at the general store. Contact Solitude Mountain Resort for more information: (801) 534-1400, www.skisolitude.com.

Dogs are not allowed in the Big Cottonwood Canyon Watershed. Do not approach or harass wildlife; animals can be unpredictable and dangerous.

The Rides (easiest to hardest)

Trail No. 1: Roundhouse Road (easy, tech 2), 2.9 miles

This is the easiest route from the top of Sunrise Lift to the

Solitude Mountain Resort

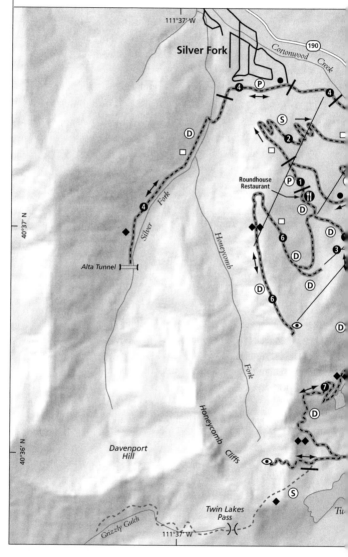

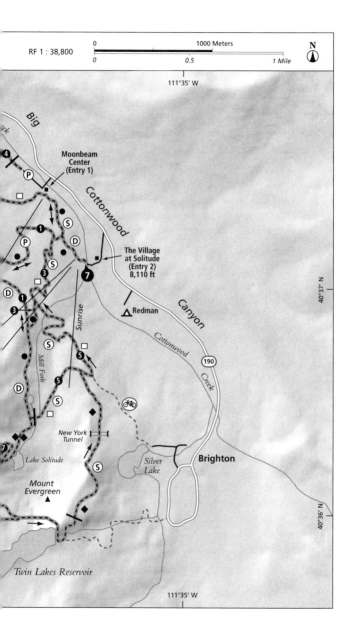

RF 1 : 38,800

0   1000 Meters

0   0.5   1 Mile

N

111°35' W

Big

Cottonwood

Moonbeam
Center
(Entry 1)

The Village
at Solitude
(Entry 2)
8,110 ft

▲ Redman

Canyon

Cottonwood

Creek

190

40°37' N

Sunrise

Mill Fork

New York
Tunnel

Lake Solitude

Silver
Lake

Brighton

Mount
Evergreen ▲

40°36' N

Twin Lakes Reservoir

111°35' W

base. It begins with a touch of singletrack, links to a mellow dirt road, and culminates with a brisk descent on a paved lane.

0.0   Exit Sunrise Lift onto singletrack and stay left/straight at the junction with Trail No. 5. Cross the small meadow under Summit Lift and go right on the main service road. Coast and pedal lightly on the smooth, packed dirt-and-sand road under Powderhorn and Apex Lifts.

1.5   Pass Roundhouse Restaurant. The dirt road turns to a paved lane.

1.9   Bend right under Eagle Express Lift and descend the road under Moonbeam Lift. Parts are steep, so control your speed and be aware of ascending mountain bikers and hikers.

2.9   Arrive back at the Village base for another ride up Sunrise Lift.

Trail No. 3: Apex (moderately easy, tech 2+ to 3+), 2.3 miles

As Chef Emeril Lagasse would say, "Kick it up a notch!" This is the "easiest" singletrack route to the base, although there are some tricky bits along the way.

0.0   Exit Sunrise Lift onto singletrack and stay left/straight at the junction with Trail No. 5. Cross the small meadow under Summit Lift and go right on the main service road. Coast and pedal lightly on the smooth, packed dirt-and-sand road.

1.0   Fork right on Trail No. 3. This short, easy path links to Trail No. 5, where the fun begins. The singletrack curves downhill under Powderhorn and Apex Lifts, dodging into the trees and crossing ski runs. There's not a lot of pedaling involved, but the bumpy, twisty trail will keep you engaged. Watch out for a set of switchbacks as you near the bottom; they can be eroded and rough.

2.0   Exit to the paved Roundhouse Road and descend.

2.3   Arrive back at the Village base for another ride up Sunrise Lift.

Trail No. 4: Silver Fork Canyon (moderate, tech 2), 4.6 miles

Escape the lift-served area and wander up a peaceful, stream-fed canyon to the old Alta Tunnel and back.

- **0.0** From the Village (entry 2), take the doubletrack past the lifts at the base area and to the paved Roundhouse access road. Pick up the singletrack near a gate on the road and zigzag down the mellow ski run underneath Link Lift.
- **0.5** Pedal across the parking lot at Moonbeam Center and pass the base of Eagle Express Lift. There you'll find a paved lane entering the conifers.
- **1.0** Veer left on a dirt doubletrack and head up Silver Fork Canyon.
- **1.5** Cross the creek and climb steadily up the canyon alongside the creek.
- **2.3** Arrive at the old Alta Tunnel. Turn around and retrace your tracks.
- **4.6** Arrive back at the Village at Solitude.

Trail No. 2: Serenity (moderate, tech 2 to 4), 4 miles

Ready for a singletrack adventure? This route links to an exciting singletrack descent that takes you across the lower mountain to Moonbeam Center. You close the loop with a mellow climb back to the Village.

- **0.0** Exit Sunrise Lift onto singletrack and stay left/straight at the junction with Trail No. 5. Cross the small meadow under Summit Lift and go right on the main service road. Coast and pedal lightly on the smooth, packed dirt-and-sand road under Powderhorn and Apex Lifts.
- **1.9** Pass Roundhouse Restaurant and fork left under Eagle Express Lift onto Trail No. 2. A rock-and-roll descent on a narrow trail takes you down to Moonbeam Center. Tight turns, boulders, and long traverses accent the trail.

3.4 Pass Moonbeam Center and climb gradually on the single-track under Link Lift.

4.0 Arrive back at the Village base for another ride up Sunrise Lift.

Trail No. 5: Kruz'r (moderately strenuous, tech 3 to 4+), 3.3 miles

This trail is the cornerstone of Solitude's trail system. Rippin' fast straightaways, serpentine curves, a short climb, and a bomber descent make it a thrill a minute.

0.0 Exit Sunrise Lift onto singletrack and fork right onto Trail No. 5 for a beautiful traverse under Sunrise Lift. Don't bobble on the few rocks or roots because all eyes from above are on you.

0.6 Fork left to continue on Trail No. 5. (The SolBright Trail to Silver Lake at Brighton is for hikers.) The fast straightaway coupled with rough tread require focused bike handling. After crossing under the lift and climbing briefly through the trees, fork left on a doubletrack and climb more steeply, then fork right onto singletrack.

1.9 Fork right at the junction with Trail No. 3 to continue on Trail No. 5. Drop into the timber and pass the yurt. The trail twists through stands of aspens and traverses ski runs. Kick into high gear and race as fast as your dare, but watch out for the final switchbacks; they're rugged and can topple an overzealous biker.

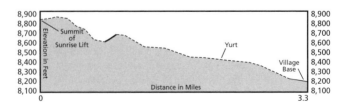

2.8	Intersect the paved service road and take it downhill to the right.
3.3	Arrive back at the Village base for another ride up Sunrise Lift.

Trail No. 6: Powderhorn Lift Road (strenuous, tech 4), 6.4 miles

This no-holds-barred climb is for riders with ultra-low gears and billy goat genes.

0.0	Exit Sunrise Lift onto singletrack and stay left/straight at the junction with Trail No. 5. Cross the small meadow under Summit Lift and go right on the main service road. Coast and pedal lightly on the smooth, packed dirt-and-sand road under Powderhorn and Apex Lifts.
1.5	After passing under Moonbeam Lift and just before Round-house Restaurant, fork left on Trail No. 6 and shift down to your low gears. Catch your breath after the road bends right and absorb the growing view of Solitude and Big Cotton-wood Canyon.
2.3	The gravel-and-rock road bends left just after passing under Eagle Express Lift. If you thought the climb was tough so far, then take a look at what lies ahead. The chunky-rock road arcs upward, passes the summit of Eagle Express Lift, and steepens more. Pedal what you can and walk the rest.
3.2	Reach the summit of Powderhorn Lift. The views are breath-taking, that is, if you have any breath left. Use caution on the descent because the loose rocks in the road can make han-dling sketchy.
4.9	Return to Roundhouse Restaurant and go left on the main road, which turns to a paved lane, and descend swiftly.
6.4	Arrive back at the Village base for another ride up Sunrise Lift.

Trail No. 7: Summit Lift Road (extremely strenuous, tech 4), 6 miles

Ride to the top of Summit Lift (elevation 10,025 feet) and you'll have something to brag about. You'll gain 1,000 feet (from the top of Sunrise Lift) in about 1.5 miles. Do the math; it's steep. If you keep going past the top, then you can climb all the way to Twin Lakes Pass for competing views of Little and Big Cottonwood Canyons. The return flight on upper SolBright Trail is exciting, to say the least.

0.0   Exit Sunrise Lift onto singletrack and stay left/straight at the junction with Trail No. 5. Cross the small meadow under Summit Lift.

0.5   Go left on the Summit Lift Road. Without mercy the road angles skyward, and you'll have to power stroke in your lowest gear over packed and loose tread.

1.5   The road levels a bit and comes to a ridge that separates Solitude from Brighton ski area. Twin Lakes Reservoir is below. Go right and keep chugging to the summit of, er, Summit Lift for full bragging rights.

2.0   Reach the top of Summit Lift. Give yourself a big pat on the back—you burly, mon! The heart of the central Wasatch Range unfolds before you. You're eye-to-eye with craggy peaks, and you peer into a valley that once housed a glacier. Across the canyon the Wasatch Crest Trail rolls along the ridge to Mill Creek Canyon.

2.5   Return to the ridgetop viewpoint of Twin Lakes and link to SolBright Trail. The doubletrack drops quickly past the lake, where it narrows to singletrack. Wrap around the timbered flank of Mount Evergreen and pass the defunct New York Tunnel. Trail conditions can be dicey, so get ready for a wild descent.

3.7   Intersect the lower SolBright Trail to Silver Lake and go left to connect with Trail No. 5. A fast straightaway over rough tread requires focused bike handling. After crossing under the lift and climbing briefly through the trees, fork left on a doubletrack and climb more steeply, then fork right on singletrack.

4.8 Fork right at the junction with Trail No. 3 to continue on Trail No. 5. Drop into the timber and pass the yurt. The trail twists through stands of aspens and traverses ski runs. Kick into high gear and race as fast as your dare, but watch out for the final switchbacks; they're rugged and can topple an overzealous biker.

5.7 Intersect the paved service road and take it downhill to the right.

6.0 Arrive back at the Village base for another ride up Sunrise Lift. Nah! Head straight to the bar and pound a cold one. You earned it.

8 Little Cottonwood Canyon Trail

This is a challenging jaunt that is scenic and historic. The trail blends smooth-rolling doubletrack and singletrack with short, steep, rough hills, so you'll get a solid workout in just over a half hour's time. Although the canyon's busy highway is a stone's throw away, the creek's churning white water and thick riparian growth provide a natural buffer from the intrusions of civilization. The trail follows a modern-day hydroelectric pipeline, which was the same route as a railroad line that served Alta during its mining heyday in the late 1800s. Granite from the canyon's slopes were the building blocks for the Salt Lake Temple of the Church of Jesus Christ of Latterday Saints, built during the mid-1800s. Mountain goats inhabit the canyon's ledgy south slopes, and rock climbers perform technical moves on huge boulders edging the trail.

Start: Temple Quarry Nature Trail parking lot at the mouth of Little Cottonwood Canyon.

Distance: 6.4-mile out-and-back.

Gain: 1,140 feet.

Physical difficulty: Moderate. Although the trail is only 3.2 miles long, it contains short, stiff climbs and sections of rough tread, often both at the same time. It might be a handful for first timers who possess only basic skills, but your skill level will improve multifold with each ride.

Technical difficulty: 2 to 4+. The "Jekyll and Hyde" trail has smooth flat stretches (tech 2) and steep choppy hills (tech 4). You'll need strong legs and sharp handling to make it through the rough parts or a willingness to walk briefly. The descent is exciting, to say the least.

Trail surface: Doubletrack with a touch of singletrack.

Season: March through November. Midday during midsummer is unbearably hot, when temperatures can near 100 degrees.

Land status: USFS Salt Lake Ranger District and parcels of private property.

Maps: USGS 1:24,000: Draper and Dromedary Peak, Utah.

Finding the trailhead: From Interstate 215 take exit 6 (6200 South, Ski Areas). Travel east on 6200 South, then south on Wasatch Boulevard and Highway 210. Follow signs for Alta and Snowbird to Little Cottonwood Canyon. Turn right at the canyon's flashing billboard and park at the Temple Quarry Nature Trail.

Know before you go: Parts of the trail cross private property, so stay on the designated route to avoid trespassing. Do not wade or swim in Little Cottonwood Creek because the current can be dangerously swift. Dogs are not allowed on the trail because it is within the Little Cottonwood Canyon Watershed. Descend cautiously, and yield to hikers and ascending mountain bikers.

The Ride

0.0 From the Temple Quarry Nature Trail parking lot, head up the sandy track at the east end of the lot.

0.7 Cross a paved road that accesses the canyon's highway to the left. Follow trail markers past the hydroelectric plant and go through a gate.

1.1 Cross a footbridge over Little Cottonwood Creek.

1.4 Pass an old pavilion on the right. The huge granite boulders alongside the trail lure sport rock climbers. The trail steepens and roughens, flattens and smooths, and then steepens and

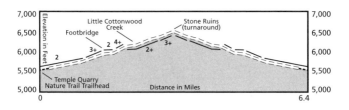

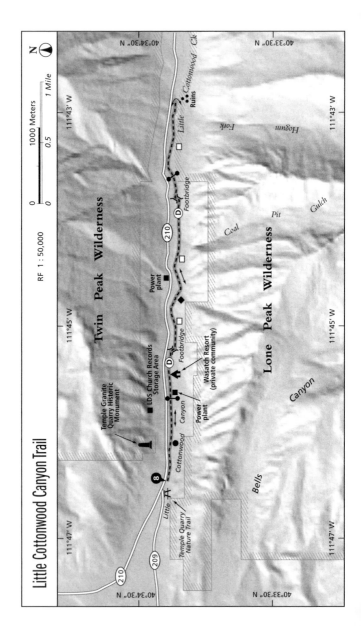

Little Cottonwood Canyon Trail

RF 1 : 50,000

N

1000 Meters

0   0.5   1 Mile

Twin Peak Wilderness

111°45' W

111°43' W

40°34'30" N

Little Cottonwood Ck

Ruins

Little Cottonwood Ck

Fork

Hogum

210

Footbridge

Coal

Pit

Gulch

Power plant

Temple Granite Quarry Historic Monument

LDS Church Records Storage Area

Footbridge

Wasatch Resort (private community)

Lone Peak Wilderness

Power plant

Cottonwood Canyon

Little Cottonwood

8

Temple Quarry Nature Trail

Bells

Canyon

210

209

111°47' W

111°47' W

111°45' W

40°33'30" N

40°33'30" N

roughens even more. This is the toughest hill, so gear down and pump hard or dismount and stretch your legs.

1.9 Cross a small boardwalk over a tributary to the main creek and stay right. The left fork exits to the highway. There are lots of shady picnic spots through here.

2.5 Pop a huge wheelie or dismount to hop onto a hefty bridge over Little Cottonwood Creek.

2.7 Enjoy easy pedaling on smooth trail and then go around a gate. Stay straight on the gravelly lane and power up one more hill. Just beyond the gate a trail forks left and exits to the highway. If you've had enough dirt for the day, then bail out and zoom down the road to the trailhead.

3.2 The trail ends at the creek's edge opposite some old stone ruins. Enjoy the return flight down the trail; you earned it.

6.4 Arrive back at the parking lot.

9 **Snowbird Resort**

During summer there's always a good reason to visit Snowbird: hiking, sightseeing, dining, music, or partying. Mountain biking, too. Novice riders to experts and cross-country purists to downhill cruisers will find a variety of trails, from the moderate-rated "Bird" Trail to the hardy Gad Valley Loop to the lung-crushing, leg-grinding Peruvian Gulch Trail hill climb. And if gravity is your friend, then the twelve-minute tram ride to Hidden Peak will net you a 2,200-foot descent. So beat the heat of the Salt Lake Valley and freshen your spirit at Snowbird.

Start: Snowbird Resort, 6.6 miles up Little Cottonwood Canyon.
Distance: Varies.
Gain: Up to 3,000 feet.
Physical difficulty: Moderate to extremely strenuous. With a base elevation of 8,000 feet, even the moderately easy Mountain Bike–Specific "Bird" Trail is tough for novice riders and flatlanders. From there it's all uphill, literally, on the moderately strenuous Gad Valley Loop or the gonzo Peruvian Gulch Trail to Hidden Peak. The latter is the route of the annual Mountain Bout bike race and is as tough as mountain biking gets in this neck of the woods. Even coasting down from the top is no easy task because of high elevations and rough trails.
Technical difficulty: 3 to 4. There's a bit of everything at Snowbird, from packed dirt singletracks to rock-riddled doubletracks. High elevation will have novice riders especially challenged.
Trail surface: Singletrack and doubletrack.
Season: July to mid-October, weather permitting.
Land status: USFS Salt Lake Ranger District and Snowbird Ski and Summer Resort.
Maps: USGS 1:24,000: Dromedary Peak, Utah. A trail map is available at Snowbird or www.snowbird.com.

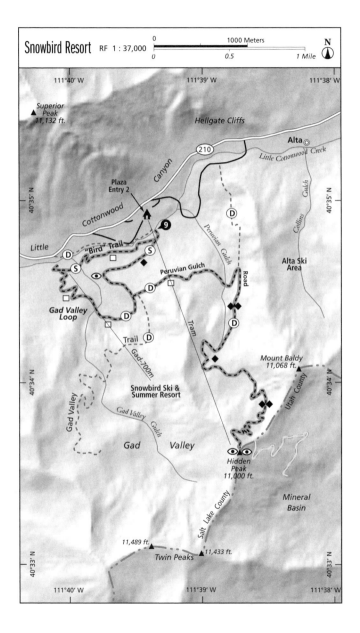

Snowbird Resort   RF 1 : 37,000

Superior Peak 11,132 ft.

Hellgate Cliffs

Alta

210

Little Cottonwood Creek

Little Cottonwood Canyon

Plaza Entry 2

Peruvian Gulch

Collins Gulch

Alta Ski Area

"Bird" Trail

Gad Valley Loop

Peruvian Gulch Road

Gad-700m. Trail

Snowbird Ski & Summer Resort

Tram

Mount Baldy 11,068 ft.

Utah County

Gad Valley

Gad Valley Gulch

Gad Valley

Hidden Peak 11,000 ft.

Salt Lake County

Mineral Basin

11,489 ft.

11,433 ft.

Twin Peaks

Finding the trailhead: From Interstate 215 take exit 6 (6200 South, Ski Areas). Travel east on 6200 South, then south on Wasatch Boulevard and Highway 210. Follow signs for Alta and Snowbird. Snowbird Ski and Summer Resort is 6.6 miles up Little Cottonwood Canyon from the flashing billboard. Take entry level 2 for the Plaza and tram.

Know before you go: Trails are open every day free of charge. The tram operates every day from 11:00 A.M. to 5:00 P.M. Lift prices: adults: $10 for one ride, $16 for all day; children (age 7 to 16): $8 for one ride, $10 for all day; children six years and under: free. For more information visit www.snowbird.com or call (800) 232-9542.

Dogs are not allowed at Snowbird Resort or in the Little Cottonwood Canyon Watershed.

The Rides

The "Bird" Trail (moderate, tech 3), 2 miles

The Mountain Bike–Specific "Bird" Trail takes you from the Plaza to Gad Valley on a near-level singletrack, but you'll have to negotiate a pair of challenging switchbacks. Chances are good that you'll spy wildlife along the way.

- **0.0** From the Plaza cross the bridge over Little Cottonwood Creek and descend the dirt service road to the right.
- **0.1** Fork left onto a doubletrack signed for GAD CHAIRS and climb about 100 yards.
- **0.2** Fork right on the "Bird" Trail. Hop over some roots, scoot around some rocks, and squeeze between the trees. Cross Big Emma ski run, bank down the choppy switchbacks, and cross a footbridge over a creek.
- **0.7** Cross the Gad Valley Trail (doubletrack) under the Gad chairs and continue on singletrack.
- **1.0** Descend a touch to the junction with the White Pine access trail, which forks left. Turn around and retrace your tracks, or

curve right, descend to the base of the Gad chairs, and take the service road back up to the Plaza.

2.0 Arrive back at the Plaza.

Gad Valley Loop (moderately strenuous, tech 3+), 2.4 miles

Course of the Intermountain Cup's annual Mountain Bout race, Gad Valley Loop combines a heart-pounding climb and a screaming descent on singletrack and doubletrack through Snowbird's mid-mountain elevations.

0.0 From the plaza cross the bridge over Little Cottonwood Creek, take a couple of deep breaths, and attack the Dick Bass Highway Trail at full force. The sharp, bouldery entry ramp is the toughest part of the upcoming climb. You'll gain elevation quickly and come eye-to-eye with the white-and-gray-banded Hellgate Cliffs across the canyon. Superior Peak rises high overhead.

0.5 The trail bends left and rises above Big Emma ski run.

0.8 Intersect Gad Valley Trail (doubletrack) and take it right across Big Emma ski run. The climbing is all but done. Kick in the afterburners and freewheel as fast as you dare, but be careful rounding the turns because the loose gravel can slide under your wheels like ball bearings.

1.8 Turn right on the "Bird" Trail. Cross a footbridge over a creek, scamper up the two choppy switchbacks, and cruise easily on solid singletrack.

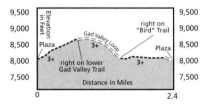

2.3 Intersect a doubletrack and take it left and downhill. Fork right on another service road alongside the creek toward the Plaza.

2.4 Arrive back at the Plaza.

Peruvian Gulch Trail (extremely strenuous, tech 3+), 4 miles

Hill climbs don't come much tougher than the one to Snowbird's Hidden Peak. And those who get there first during the annual Mountain Bout race are crowned king/queen of the mountain. Gaining nearly 3,000 feet in 4 miles, the average grade is nearly 14 percent—and that's steep. Or forget the climb, ride the tram to the top, and coast the whole way down. Even so, the descent is rated moderately strenuous because of high elevation, steep grades, and choppy doubletracks.

0.0 From the plaza cross the bridge over Little Cottonwood Creek, take a couple of deep breaths, and attack the Dick Bass Highway Trail at full force. The sharp, bouldery entry ramp will jump-start your heart, and the steady grade thereafter will keep your pulse pegged. If you struggle here, you might want to reconsider going the distance.

0.8 Turn left on Gad Valley Trail, pass the top of Wilbere lift, and fork left on Rothman Way ski run where Gad Valley Trail forks right. The grade subsides, only a bit, giving you a chance to

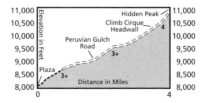

tuck your heart back into your chest. The shade from the tall conifers is a welcome relief.

1.5 Fork right on the Peruvian Gulch Road shortly after passing under Peruvian lift. Take more deep breaths because now the climb really begins.

2.4 Soft-pedal as the road flattens and curves across Chip's Run. The respite is all too short, though. Round a left switch-back and get back to work.

3.0 Welcome another short respite as the road crosses the basin beneath the Cirque. Look up the craggy headwall and you'll see that your mountaintop goal is still 1,000 vertical feet away.

3.7 Start the final switchbacks. Put your pedal to the metal to keep your rear wheel from slipping out on the coarse gravel and loose tread.

3.9 Round the last turn and keep pumping hard as you crest the Cirque headwall. Don't falter now because there's a tram full of gawkers directly overhead.

4.0 Reach the top of Hidden Peak. Milk the moment for all its worth while accepting congratulations from the dumb-struck tourists milling around. Don't whisk away too soon; the views are among the finest in the Wasatch. But when you're ready, point your front wheel back down the road with cool, calm conviction. Don't even think about riding the tram down!

For those of you who cheated and took the tram to the top, just reverse the ride log above. Use caution descending because the road is steep and the tread can be loose dirt and rock (tech 3 to 4). Ascending hikers and mountain bikers have the right of way.

10 Albion Basin Summer Road

Alta Ski Area is a locals' favorite even after the "Greatest Snow on Earth" has melted. During summer you can get an up-close look at the terrain that has made Alta legendary, but from the seat of your bike. Rough-cut peaks silhouette the skyline in all directions, and wildflowers as vibrant and varied as a painter's palette blanket the alpine meadows.

The ride is a piece of cake, except for the fact that it starts at nearly 9,000 feet. If you go slow and take breaks to catch your breath, then the canyon's glacial architecture will seem to swallow you whole. From the turnaround point at the campground, you can hike the easy, mile-long trail to Cecret Lake for a midday siesta. Since traffic is light and slow, it's a good choice for couples and for families with children.

Start: Alta Ski Area, 8.7 miles up Little Cottonwood Canyon Road.
Distance: 6-mile out-and-back.
Gain: 800 feet.
Physical difficulty: Moderately easy. The road's gradual, steady rise is rated easy on a relative scale, but since the trailhead is at nearly 9,000 feet, flatlanders and first-timers will feel their lungs squeezed from the thin air.

Technical difficulty: 2. The two-lane road is mostly smooth-packed dirt, but you may encounter some gravel and washboards.
Trail surface: All-weather dirt road.
Season: Late June through September.
Land status: USFS Salt Lake Ranger District.
Maps: USGS 1:24,000: Brighton and Dromedary Peak, Utah.

Finding the trailhead: From Interstate 215 take exit 6 (6200 South, Ski Areas). Travel east on 6200 South, then south on Wasatch Boulevard and Highway 210. Follow signs for Alta and Snowbird.

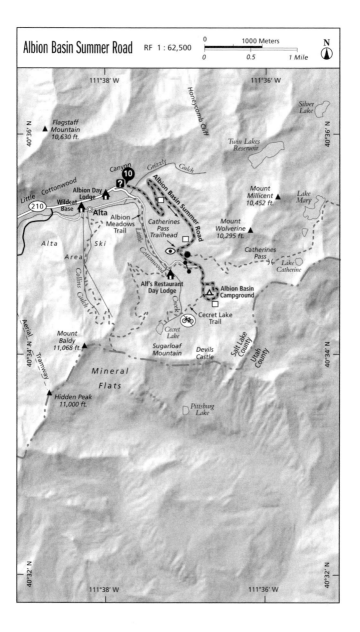

Albion Basin Summer Road

RF 1 : 62,500

Drive 8.7 miles up Little Cottonwood Canyon Road from the flashing billboard at the canyon's entrance to the end of the pavement at Alta Ski Area's Albion base.

Know before you go: Be prepared for rapidly changing alpine weather. Summer cabin areas are private property. Ride only designated trails, do not ride through meadows, and do not shortcut switchbacks. Stay to the right side of the road, and be aware of motorists, who are more frequent on weekends. Dogs are not allowed in the Little Cottonwood Canyon Watershed.

The Ride

0.0 From the end of the pavement at Alta's Albion Basin base area, go past the information booth and head up the dirt Albion Basin Summer Road.

0.6 Switchback to the left.

1.1 Switchback to the right.

2.1 Reach the Catherines Pass Trailhead and parking area. Take a break and check out the interpretive plaque that outlines Alta's topography. Most striking is the tilted ridge of dark gray limestones called Devils Castle, which seals off the basin to the south. Since there is no lift access to the Castle, skiers have to traverse long distances with their skis on to "get the good" on an epic powder day.

2.7–3.3 Ride the half-mile loop around Albion Basin Campground in either direction, or lock your bike and hike the Cecret Lake Trail (bikes not allowed); then retrace your tracks down the road to the trailhead.

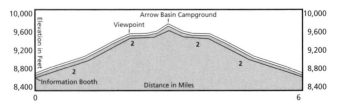

Honorable Mentions

Here are some rides that missed the cut but are worthy of mention. Get out and ride, take some notes, and report back.

Upper Mill Creek Canyon/Great Western Trail: If you made easy work of Big Water Trail, then branch off onto the Great Western Trail in Upper Mill Creek Canyon. The trail rises 3 miles to the Mill Creek Canyon Divide, where you can turn around or pursue a variety of options incorporating the Wasatch Crest Trail.

Mill D North Fork Trail/Desolation Trail: Got legs? If so, put them to the test on the 3.7-mile climb to Lake Desolation in Big Cottonwood Canyon. Begin at Reynolds Flat and start humping like a good soldier up Mill D North Fork Trail. Then grin and bear the hike-a-bike past the Desolation Trail junction. A steady grind takes you to Lake Desolation. The return flight is a thrill a minute.

Bonneville Shoreline Trail (Draper): Years in the making, the Draper section of the BST is finally being completed through Lower Corner Canyon, which had been a longtime stalling point. Now you can ride about 8 miles from Upper Corner Canyon Road straight through to Point of the Mountain Flight Park, where hang gliders take to flight. If you hook up with the 1.5-mile North Maple Hollow Trail, you can climb to the Suncrest Development on the Traverse Mountains ridge and pursue more trails, like the South Maple Hollow Trail.

Upper Corner Canyon Road (Draper): Want to get some easy miles under your belt before hitting the mountain singletracks? Then hit the dirt on Upper Corner Canyon Road. A moderate 3.8-mile climb takes you across the Draper foothills to the Traverse Mountains where you can sight north and south along the Wasatch Range. Veer off onto the BST to test your singletrack prowess.

Rose Canyon: Tucked away in the far southwest corner of Salt Lake County, Rose Canyon is a secret stash for dirt riders. Check out the steep climbs in Yellow Fork and Water Fork. Burly!

Road
Biking
Rides

11 Saltair

If you close your eyes, this ride is as mundane as slogging out tedious midwinter miles on your trainer in a windowless basement, for there is nary a pimple of a hill along the way to offer any terrain variance. Open, your eyes will fall upon sights that define northern Utah. Rows of towering block-faulted mountains bound the post–Ice Age Great Salt Lake, and a compact but distinctive city skyline marks the hub of a sprawling metro boasting a million-plus inhabitants. From the ride's turnaround at the Great Salt Lake State Marina, you can whiff the lake's salty air and gaze to distant islands and mountains, and the Ottoman-style Saltair Pavilion along the way gives the ride an oddball Middle Eastern flair.

The ride begins on the Airport Bike Path, turns through a business center, and strikes a beeline west along the Inter-state 80 frontage road, which you'll likely have all to yourself. Spin casually or practice a team time trial on this one.

Start: Airport Bike Path at Salt Lake International Airport.
Distance: 31.4-mile out-and-back.
Gain: About 50 feet, no lie!
Physical difficulty: Moderate. Dorothy would think she was riding across the plains of Kansas because road rides don't get any flatter. Still, 30-plus miles is nothing to scoff at. The greatest challenge might be battling a wind, which can be bothersome blow-

ing off the lake, up the valley, or around the Oquirrh Mountains.
Margin of comfort: Fair to good overall. You start out on designated bike lanes around the airport and through the International Center. The I-80 frontage road has no shoulder but it sees little traffic. From Saltair to the marina, the road has no shoulder and is lined with cement barriers where margin of comfort is poor but traffic is still light.

Season: March through November and throughout winter when the roads are dry and you can brave the cold.

Maps: USGS 1:24,000: North Salt Lake and Saltair, Utah.

Finding the trailhead: From Salt Lake City take Interstate 15 north then I-80 west for the airport. Exit to Redwood Road, go right/north, and turn left/west onto North Temple Street. Where North Temple bends left (becoming Highway 186) and passes under Interstate 215, stay straight/due west on North Temple proper and go under I-215. Cross 2200 West and park at the end of the road at the gated fence. The parking area accommodates a half-dozen vehicles. The best approach by bike to the trailhead is to ride through Salt Lake City on 800 South (becomes Indiana Avenue/850 South), which has a bike lane and offers a safe crossing under I-15. Turn right onto Redwood and go north to North Temple Street, then turn left.

Know before you go: The Airport Bike Path crosses a "secured area," so don't go deviating from the route. You really can't anyhow, because the route is fenced. Parts of the I-80 frontage road are rough, cracked pavement. Watch your line and be alert to traffic if you must veer to avoid a hazard. Saltair has a gift shop, snack bar, and restroom. The marina has a restroom, water fountain, snack stand, and soda vending machine. The Airport Bike Path is open April through September from 5:00 A.M. to 10:00 P.M. and October through March from 7:00 A.M. to 7:00 P.M. For emergencies call the airport control center: (801) 575-2405.

The Ride

0.0 Don't be intimidated by the guard station and penitentiary-style fence at the trailhead parking area. Just go through the gate to the left and hop onto the Airport Bike Path. The bike path runs alongside the edge of a narrow road that goes around the airport's southern perimeter. Cross the flight landing/takeoff path, but don't stop to watch the jets overhead because signs along the road prohibit it.

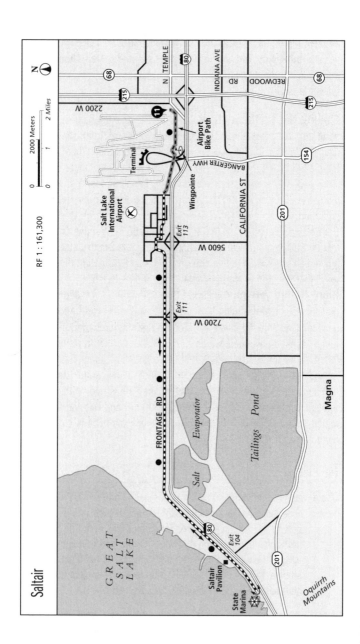

Saltair

RF 1 : 161,300

N

1.0 Go through another gate and exit to a road at a T-junction. Go right, following the bike path. Left accesses Wingpointe Golf Course.

1.3 Cross the road to link to the continued bike lane, which is now separated from the roadway. The bike lane follows a canal and on the south edge of the airport parking lots.

1.7 The trail bends left and runs along the airport entrance road.

1.8 Go through a gate, turn right onto the paved golf course cart path, and ride through two tunnels that go under the airport entrance/exit roads.

2.0 After exiting the second tunnel, veer right toward hole number 12 and go through yet another gate. Now the lane runs along the north edge of the golf course.

2.2 The trail splits; stay right/straight.

2.8 Pass a second flight landing/takeoff path, and exit through one last gate onto a service road just north of Microtel Suites (motel). Go right onto Tommy Thompson Road (4700 West) and then bend left onto Wiley Post Drive (250 North).

3.2 Cross Wright Brothers Drive at a stoplight and ride through the International Center. Be aware of traffic through the business district, as not all intersections are four-way stops.

4.1 Turn right onto Admiral Byrd Road (5480 West).

4.3 Turn left onto Amelia Earhart Drive (gas station/convenience store and sub shop at the junction).

4.4 Cross 5600 West. The shoulder is now absent.

4.5 Turn left onto Apollo Road (5650 West) and trade the busi-

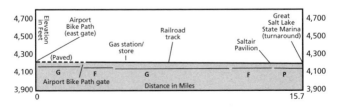

ness center for open spaces where cattle often graze. There is no white line or shoulder, but the wide, two-lane road sees little traffic. The road bends right and runs parallel to I-80, which is a stone's throw away. The grassy fields on the right yield to the mudflat shoreline of the Great Salt Lake. In the distance Frary Peak marks the high point of Antelope Island's craggy spine.

5.4 Cross a railroad track. To your left and across I-80, the Oquirrh Mountains rise to impressive proportions with Kessler and Farnsworth Peaks topping out at about 9,000 feet.

6.7 Cross 7200 West at exit 111 off I-80. The road narrows and the surface is cracked, patched, and choppy cement, making for a rougher ride. Be kind to those on your rear wheel by pointing out road hazards, or back off from the lead riders because you may have to make sudden moves to avoid the rough stuff. The road makes a beeline west for as far as you can see.

8.6 The road reverts to smooth asphalt and the shoulder is 1 foot. This is an excellent opportunity to practice riding in a paceline since traffic is minimal and sight lines are infinite.

11.3 The road bends southwest and points toward the huge smokestack of the Kennecott copper smelter on the north end of the Oquirrh Mountains. More interesting is the conspicuous bench on the mountains' foothills that marks the wave-cut shoreline of ancient Lake Bonneville; the Stansbury Mountains shape the western skyline behind the Oquirrhs. The north lane is now lined with a cement barrier. The shoulder is less than 1 foot, but margin of comfort is still fair to good because of light traffic. The Saltair Pavilion, still nearly 2 miles away, floats on the lake's shore like a Turkish mosque in a mirage.

13.9 Reach the Saltair Pavilion (exit 104 off I-80). Built in 1893 by Mormon businessmen who envisioned it to become the "Coney Island of the West," the amusement park and pavilion entertained more than a million visitors until fire destroyed it in 1925. Since rebuilt, it serves as a concert venue and dance hall. Continue on the frontage road to reach the marina. Now the road is lined with cement barriers on both sides, and you will be forced to ride in the traffic lane as there is no shoulder. Margin of comfort is poor, so ride cautiously. Even a layman of geology can see how tectonic forces have crunched the earth's crust and upended layers of sedimentary rocks at the base of the nearby Oquirrh Mountains.

15.7 Reach the Great Salt Lake State Marina and turnaround point. Don't be hasty in your departure. Take time to step onto the observation deck and muse at the stark beauty of this great landlocked puddle. If the lake was deep fresh water, Salt Lake would be a veritable oasis, but alas, the shallow, murky lake's main claim to fame is brine shrimping. Return the way you came. All the while the Wasatch Range from Ogden's Ben Lomond to Salt Lake's Lone Peak provides constant visual entertainment, and the downtown Salt Lake skyline grows majestically.

31.4 Arrive back at the trailhead.

12 North Salt Lake Loop

This north valley loop links Salt Lake City with North Salt Lake on a tour of striking "diversity." The bulk of the loop follows busy city streets and highways where the shoulder is absent and high-speed traffic is moderate to heavy. You'll cruise past industrial complexes, gravel pits, airports, and oil refineries. And there is nary a hill to speak of. So why bother? Despite these blights of civilization, the first and last legs of the loop follow bike lanes through quaint ethnic neighborhoods and across open spaces where cattle graze. The miles are respectable, you can spin at a good tempo the whole way, and the last mile on the Jordan River Parkway is a pleasant way to wind down.

Start: Constitution Park at 300 North and 1200 West.
Distance: 20.5-mile loop.
Gain: 300 feet, if that.
Physical difficulty: Moderate. There are no hills to speak of. The hardest part might be tackling a headwind.
Margin of comfort: Poor to fair. About half of the loop follows bike lanes on city streets, but margin of comfort is only fair because of moderate to heavy traffic and tight lanes. Beck Street is downright dangerous for bicycles, but it's the only way between Salt Lake City and North Salt Lake. The frontage road takes you out of the danger zone briefly. Roads in North Salt Lake don't have bike lanes, so you'll be brushing shoulders with motorists.
Season: March through November and throughout winter when roads are dry and you can brave the cold.
Maps: USGS 1:24,000: Farmington and Salt Lake City North, Utah.

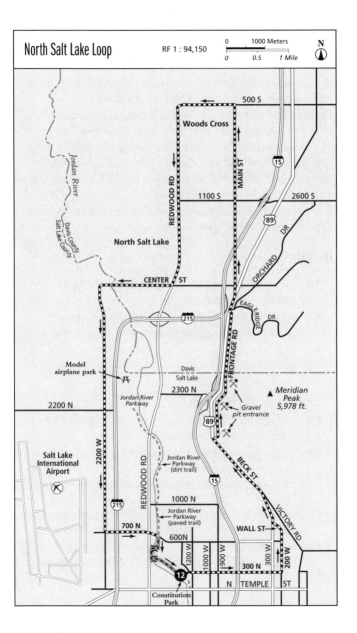

North Salt Lake Loop

RF 1 : 94,150

0   1000 Meters
0   0.5   1 Mile

N

500 S

Woods Cross

REDWOOD RD

MAIN ST

I-15

1100 S

2600 S

89

ORCHARD DR

North Salt Lake

Jordan River

Davis County
Salt Lake County

CENTER ST

215

EAGLE RIDGE DR

FRONTAGE RD

Model airplane park

Davis Salt Lake

▲ **Meridian Peak** 5,978 ft.

Jordan River Parkway

2300 N

Gravel pit entrance

2200 N

89

Salt Lake International Airport

⊗

215

2200 W

REDWOOD RD

Jordan River Parkway (dirt trail)

15

BECK ST

1000 N

Jordan River Parkway (paved trail)

VICTORY RD

700 N

600 N

WALL ST

1200 W

1000 W

900 W

300 W

300 N

300 W

200 W

12

N TEMPLE ST

Constitution Park

Finding the trailhead: The loop begins at Constitution Park in the Rose Park community. From North Temple Street take 1000 West northward and turn left onto 300 North (on the north side of the Utah State Fairpark). Enter Constitution Park where 300 North bends right and becomes Clark Avenue (at about 1200 West).

Know before you go: Beck Street/U.S. Highway 89 is dangerous for bicycles because there is no shoulder on the six-lane road and high-speed traffic can be heavy. But it's the only link between Salt Lake City and North Salt Lake. Ride attentively and defensively. Sunday is the best time to ride because commercial industries are closed, thus lessening truck traffic. Portions of 500 South in North Salt Lake and Redwood Road have narrow or nonexistent shoulders, and traffic is moderate; again, ride cautiously.

The Ride

0.0 Exit Constitution Park to 300 North and take the road's bike lane east toward Salt Lake City.

1.4 Cross 300 West/US 89. (You can turn left onto 300 West if desired, but continuing on limits the time spent on this busy road.)

1.5 Turn left onto 200 West (bike lane) and ride through another old-style neighborhood.

2.2 Turn left onto Wall Street.

2.4 Turn right onto 300 West/US 89, pass Warm Springs Park (alternate trailhead), and leave Salt Lake City.

2.9 Victory Road/Highway 184 enters from the right at this stoplight and 300 West becomes Beck Street. You are entering the danger zone, as the shoulder disappears and traffic is heavy and fast on the six-lane road. Ride defensively and cautiously. Fortunately, there are no scenic distractions along this stretch other than industrial complexes and oil refineries.

4.1 At the stoplight at 1810 North just past Southern Exposure Show Club, turn right onto the frontage road at the entrance to the gravel pit and continue north. The narrow two-lane road is Salt Lake's version of the famed Paris-Roubaix, as the pavement is often rough, cracked, and potholed, and your spine will feel every bump. Traffic is light but you might encounter large trucks accessing the gravel pit. Watch your line while watching out for vehicles simultaneously. Overall, the frontage road is a safer choice than continuing on Beck Street/US 89.

6.2 Intersect US 89 and take it right. Pass Eagleridge Drive forking right and stay north on US 89.

6.4 Turn left onto Main Street. Use caution crossing traffic lanes, or go another block to the stoplight at Center Street, then go left to Main.

6.6 Cross Center Street. The shoulder on Main is less than 1 foot but the speed limit is 30 mph and traffic is light to moderate.

7.5 Use caution crossing the several sets of railroad tracks because they run at a sharp angle to your line.

8.4 Cross a single railroad track.

8.6 A WATCH FOR BICYCLES sign alongside the road might calm your nerves with the notion that motorists are in fact watching out for you. Farther on, the warehouses yield to modern and old-style residences and the riding is quite pleasant even though there is still no shoulder.

9.5 Turn left onto 500 South/Highway 68. (There's a gas station/convenience store here.) The shoulder is less than 1 foot and the speed limit is 45 mph. It's a tight squeeze for motorists and bicyclists, so ride cautiously. The road leaves

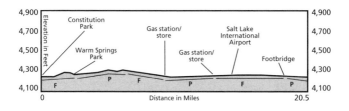

the residential areas and heads out across open spaces where cattle graze.

10.4 500 South bends south and becomes Redwood Road. This is the second of the loop's danger zones as the shoulder is less than 1 foot and the speed limit increases to 55 mph. Watch your line and watch your behind.

13.3 Turn right onto Center Street at the gas station/convenience store and ride past warehouses on the right and ranch lands on the left. There is no shoulder but traffic is light.

14.6 The road bends left/south and continues as 2200 West. Ranch houses and broad pastures give this section a country-lane feel. Although the road is posted as a bike route, there is no shoulder and the pavement can be rough, but traffic is light. Off to the right, airliners take off and land at Salt Lake International Airport. Beyond, the 9,000-foot-tall Oquirrh Mountains divide the Salt Lake Valley from the Basin and Range Province.

16.6 Cross 2200 North. Now 2200 West is a designated bike lane, although half of the lane is a cement gutter and the pavement can be choppy. Despite the bike lane, you might be forced to ride in the traffic lane. Enjoy an excellent view of the central Wasatch Range from the Salt Lake City center to Lone Peak.

18.6 Turn left onto 700 North. The so-called bike lane is barely 1 foot wide, so ride cautiously on this busy, multilane city street.

19.3 Cross Redwood Road. The bike lane disappears and margin of comfort is poor.

19.5 Turn right at the crossing signal onto the Jordan River Parkway (paved path) and breathe a sigh of relief as you curve quietly through a canopy of tall cottonwoods next to the placid stream, sans vehicles.

19.8 Take the footbridge to the river's west bank, then cross 500 North. Cross a bridge back to the east bank just north of the Utah Department of Agriculture building.

20.5 Arrive back at Constitution Park via the back door.

13 City Creek Canyon Road

Located only 1 mile from Salt Lake City's central business district, City Creek Canyon is a treasured amenity for the valley's residents. Within minutes you can escape the confines of urbanism and become immersed in a tranquil natural sanctuary. Shady picnic areas dot the banks of the bubbling creek, and an array of wildlife thrives within the brushy canyon.

The lower road to the water treatment plant rises in stairstep fashion with short, moderately pitched hills softened by gentle respites. Past the plant the road rises steadily and more steeply and summons your lowest gears on a permanent basis. It's all good. The return glide, although regulated by a 15 mph speed limit, is worth the effort.

Start: Entrance gate to City Creek Canyon Road.
Distance: 11.2-mile out-and-back.
Gain: 1,400 feet.
Physical difficulty: Moderate. The lower canyon section to the water treatment plant is moderately easy, with short hills offset by frequent respites (3.5 percent average grade); however, the upper canyon portion from the water treatment plant to Rotary Park is moderately strenuous, with a steady, steeper pitch (6.5 percent average grade).

Margin of comfort: Good. Although there is no shoulder on the narrow two-lane road, the road is biker friendly and is closed to motorists on "biker days." Still, you must be alert to canyon maintenance trucks, and more importantly to pedestrians, joggers, and other cyclists on the road, as many curves are blind.
Season: The road is open to bicyclists from 8:30 A.M. to 10:00 P.M. on odd-numbered calendar days (excluding holidays) from the last Monday of May to the last weekend of September.

City Creek Canyon Road

RF 1 : 95,600

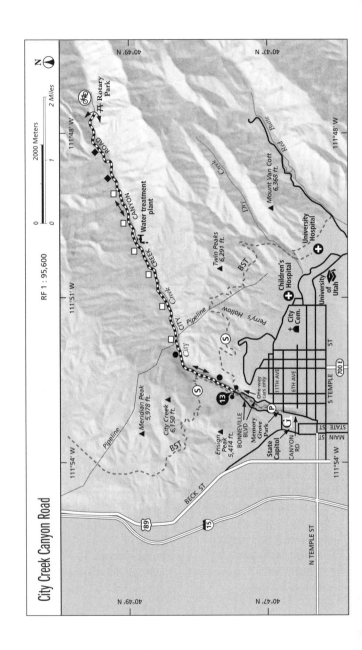

During the remainder of the year, bicyclists are allowed every day. Motorists, skateboarders, and in-line skaters are allowed on even- numbered calendar days. Pedestrians are allowed every day. **Maps:** USGS 1:24,000: Fort Douglas and North Salt Lake, Utah.

Finding the trailhead: By vehicle from the city center, take State Street north and turn right onto North Temple Street, which becomes 2nd Avenue (one-way, west to east). Turn left onto B Street and drive uphill to the intersection with 11th Avenue. Go straight onto Bonneville Boulevard, which is one-way from east to west for motorists (two-way for bicyclists and pedestrians). Drive 0.6 mile and turn right onto City Creek Canyon Road. The entrance gate and small parking area are a few hundred yards farther. You can park at the nearby Bonneville Shoreline Trailhead as well.

By bicycle from the city center, you can follow the same directions as above or access City Creek Canyon via Memory Grove Park. For the latter take State Street north and turn right onto North Temple Street (be alert to heavy traffic), then turn left immediately onto Canyon Road. Enter Memory Grove and climb gradually for 1 mile through the park to the intersection with Bonneville Boulevard/City Creek Canyon Road.

Know before you go: The canyon road speed limit is 15 mph. Citations will be issued to cyclists and motorists exceeding the speed limit. During winter months the lower road to the water treatment plant is plowed regularly but may be icy; the road above the plant is not plowed. The road above the plant is one lane with no shoulder and can be rough, cracked, and potholed pavement. Use caution, especially when descending. Be alert to other users, as the road is narrow and winding with many blind corners.

There is a water fountain at the entrance gate and at the water treatment plant. Many picnic areas have outhouses. Dogs must be leashed and are not allowed above the water treatment plant. Swimming, wading, and allowing dogs in the water are prohibited. The canyon can be very hot at midday during midsummer, with temperatures above 90 degrees.

The Ride

0.0   At the entrance gate read the canyon rules and warnings about this being bear, mountain lion, and rattlesnake country. The road welcomes you with a gentle incline to warm up on.

1.0   The road steepens a bit, and you'll start working the shifters and seeking your easier gears. Relax on the respites, then repeat. Thick riparian growth and tall deciduous trees line the creek and drape the road.

2.8   Enter the City Creek Canyon Watershed. Dogs are not allowed beyond this point.

3.2   Reach the water treatment plant. This is a good turnaround point for novice riders as the remainder is noticeably steeper. The road narrows to one lane and winds through a thick veil of brush and trees. Moss clings to the roadside boulders and banks where springs trickle from the hillside.

4.4   Enter the Rotary Park boundary, but the park itself is still a mile away. Now the road steepens to nearly 8 percent on average, and you'll be pumping hard.

5.6   Reach the end of the road at the Rotary Park pavilion. Unlike other Wasatch Front canyon roads, you can't descend City Creek with abandon. The upper road can be rough and the turns are tight and blind. Although the lower road is smooth, you must *always* anticipate other users in your lane when rounding every bend. And if you get zapped for speeding, you'll get fined! That's not to say the descent is a letdown; it's just a mellow coast through nature, not a breakneck tuck-and-glide.

11.2   Arrive back at the entrance gate.

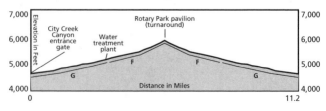

14 Bountiful Bench

If you're going to battle the high-speed, six-lane traffic on Beck Street/U.S. Highway 89 and endure the visual blight of its industrial complexes and oil refineries, then you'd might as well have a good reason. This route takes you from Salt Lake City's Liberty Park to a scenic loop on Bountiful's east bench and back, which is reason enough to ride it. But despite the long, flat, easy miles, you'd better have strong legs or ultra-low gears because Bountiful's Eagle Ridge Drive is one of the steepest climbs on the Wasatch Front. This ascent alone is the main reason to ride, or avoid, this route. The hill is only 1.8 miles long, so it's no Alpe d'Huez, but it's nothing to scoff at either. If you can't hang, then you'll suffer.

Start: Liberty Park.
Distance: 29.2-mile lariat-shaped loop.
Gain: 1,800 feet.
Physical difficulty: Moderately strenuous. Lots of flats, *but* the 1.8-mile climb up Bountiful's Eagleridge Drive is remarkably steep, maxing out at nearly 12 percent grade. Ouch!
Margin of comfort: Poor to fair overall. Bike lanes on busy streets take you through downtown Salt Lake City. The 1.5-mile stretch on Beck Street/US 89 is downright frightening for bicycles, as the shoulderless six-lane road receives heavy, high-speed traffic. But if you need or want to get between Salt Lake City and Bountiful, it's the only way. The frontage road gets you out of the danger zone, but it too warrants caution because it lacks a shoulder and gravel trucks might be encountered. The residential roads through Bountiful do not have bike lanes but are pleasant to ride because traffic is generally light and speed limits are low.
Season: March through November and throughout winter when roads are dry and you can brave the cold.

Maps: USGS 1:24,000: Bountiful Peak, Fort Douglas, Salt Lake City North, Salt Lake City South, and Sugarhouse, Utah. (Some Bountiful roads are not shown.)

Finding the trailhead: The ride begins at Liberty Park. You can enter the park on 900 South at 600 East and on 1300 South at 600 East.

Know before you go: Beck Street/US 89 is dangerous for bicycles because there is no shoulder on the six-lane road and traffic is heavy and fast. But it's the only link between Salt Lake City and Bountiful. Ride attentively and defensively. Sunday is the best time to ride because commercial industries are closed, thus lessening truck traffic.

The Ride

0.0 Exit Liberty Park at 900 South and ride north on 600 East.

0.2 Turn left onto 800 South. Traffic can be heavy on this four-lane city street but you have a designated bike lane. Be alert to doors being opened from parked cars.

1.4 Turn right onto 200 West (bike lane) and ride into downtown Salt Lake City.

2.5 At 100 South, 200 West goes through a tunnel under the Salt Palace. A sign directs you onto a wide sidewalk, which is the designated bike route and safely separates you from traffic. The bike lane resumes on 200 West north of South Temple Street and runs through a small residential area.

3.7 Turn left onto Wall Street and pass Warm Springs Park (alternate trailhead).

3.9 Turn right onto 300 West, which becomes Beck Street/US 89. As you head out of town, the wide parking lane narrows until there is no shoulder.

4.4 Pass Victory Road/Highway 184 entering from the right (stoplight). (Victory Road provides alternate access to this route from the Avenues area via 11th Avenue and Bonneville

Boulevard.) The speed limit increases to 50 mph and there is no shoulder. You are entering the danger zone; ride cautiously. Fortunately, there are no scenic distractions along this stretch other than industrial complexes and oil refineries.

5.6 At the stoplight at 1810 North just past Southern Exposure Show Club, turn right onto the frontage road at the entrance to the gravel pit and continue north. The narrow two-lane road is Salt Lake's version of the famed Paris-Roubaix, as the pavement is often rough, cracked, and potholed, and your spine will feel every bump. Traffic is light but you might encounter heavy trucks accessing the gravel pit. Watch your line while watching out for vehicles simultaneously. Overall, the frontage road is a safer choice than continuing on Beck Street/US 89.

7.7 Intersect US 89 and take it right.

7.8 Turn right onto Eagle Ridge Drive, circle the roundabout halfway, and follow the sign for the golf course. (Be alert to merging traffic.) Get ready to climb. The road tilts up and your gears shift down, and you'll exhaust your low gears in short order. The road curves uphill out of the valley and onto the ancient Lake Bonneville shoreline 800 feet above, passing ritzy custom homes along the way. Whether you're a lithe spinner or a powerhouse diesel, you'll find the savage grade to be borderline humorous.

8.7 The grade slackens. Recover, and take a second to glance back down from where you came and out across the Great Salt Lake; then the road pitches up to a crushing 12 percent for another half mile. Ouch!

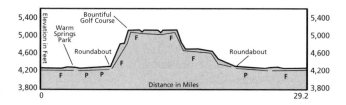

9.6 The road curves left and tops out on the edge of Eaglewood Golf Course at the northern trailhead for the Ensign Peak section of the Bonneville Shoreline Trail. Breathe a sigh of relief and spin.

10.3 Leaving Eaglewood Golf Course behind, the road becomes Bountiful Boulevard and passes trophy homes high on the Bountiful bench. There is no white line or shoulder, but the quiet, wide residential road is comfortable for bikes.

11.2 Dip downhill to Indian Springs Drive and climb briefly, then ride alongside the Bountiful Golf Course. There you'll find beautiful sights of the northern Wasatch Range with Ogden's Ben Lomond Peak poking its head over the shoulder of nearby Bountiful Peak. The Great Salt Lake and distant mountains of the Basin and Range Province sprawl out to the west.

13.4 Descend speedily to a stop sign at Mueller Park Road (1800 South). Continue north, climbing briefly but steeply along the scenic foothills.

14.3 Roll along at a fast pace past the Holbrook Canyon Trailhead (outhouse and water fountain) and past the Bountiful Temple of the Church of Jesus Christ of Latter-day Saints.

15.1 The road bends west and descends rapidly at a near 10 percent grade. This is no place to tuck-and-glide because you will have to brake hard for the stop sign at 1300 East.

15.5 *Do not* run the stop sign at 1300 East because it's only a two-way stop and cross traffic does not stop!

15.8 Turn left onto Davis Boulevard. This is a dicey turn because you must brake hard down the steep hill while signaling your left at the same time. Go easy and watch out for traffic. Davis Boulevard runs on a near level keel through an older, modest residential section of Bountiful.

16.2 Cross Center Street (Bountiful), which becomes 500 South west of Interstate 15 if you want to link to the second half of the North Salt Lake Loop.

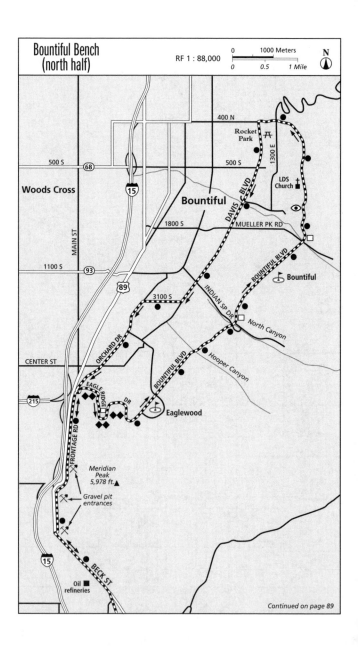

Bountiful Bench
(north half)

RF 1 : 88,000

| 0 | | 1000 Meters |
| 0 | 0.5 | 1 Mile |

N

400 N

Rocket Park

500 S

68

Woods Cross

I-15

500 S

1300 E

LDS Church

Bountiful

DAVIS BLVD

MUELLER PK RD

1800 S

Bountiful

1100 S

93

US 89

BOUNTIFUL BLVD

3100 S

INDIAN SP DR

North Canyon

ORCHARD DR

CENTER ST

BOUNTIFUL BLVD

Hooper Canyon

I-215

EAGLE RIDGE DR

Eaglewood

FRONTAGE RD

Meridian Peak
5,978 ft.

Gravel pit entrances

15

BECK ST

Oil refineries

MAIN ST

Continued on page 89

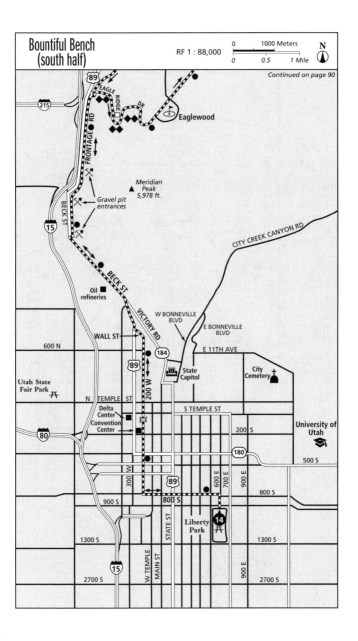

Bountiful Bench (south half)

RF 1 : 88,000

0   1000 Meters
0   0.5   1 Mile

N

Continued on page 90

89

215

Eagle Ridge Dr

Frontage Rd

Eaglewood

Beck St

Meridian Peak 5,978 ft.

Gravel pit entrances

15

City Creek Canyon Rd

Beck St

Oil refineries

Victory Rd

W Bonneville Blvd

E Bonneville Blvd

Wall St

600 N

89

184

E 11th Ave

200 W

State Capitol

City Cemetery

Utah State Fair Park

80

N Temple St

Delta Center
Convention Center

S Temple St

200 S

University of Utah

500 S

300 W

180

600 E
700 E
900 E

89

800 S

800 S

15

900 S

State St

Liberty Park

14

W Temple

Main St

1300 S

1300 S

900 E

2700 S

2700 S

19.0 Turn right onto 3100 South. There is no shoulder, but you'll be descending at the speed of traffic.

19.5 Turn left onto Orchard Drive. Traffic is generally moderate (heavy southbound at the morning rush hour and heavy northbound at the evening rush hour), and the shoulder is about 3 feet.

20.7 Cross Center Street (North Salt Lake)—following Center Street right/west will connect you with Main Street on the North Salt Lake Loop.

21.2 Return to the roundabout at Eagle Ridge Drive.

21.3 Turn left onto US 89 at the stoplight.

21.4 Use caution crossing traffic lanes to make the left turn onto the frontage road.

23.5 Exit the frontage road and turn left onto Beck Street. Ride cautiously along the busy shoulderless highway.

24.7 Go straight at the stoplight where Victory Road/Highway 184 veers left.

25.2 Turn left onto Wall Street, or stay on Beck Street/US 89 (which now becomes 300 West) and turn left onto 600 North at the stoplight and then turn right onto Wall Street. Take 200 West (bike lane) through downtown Salt Lake City, remembering to take the sidewalk through the tunnel under the Salt Palace.

27.8 Turn left onto 800 South (bike lane).

29.0 Turn right onto 600 East.

29.2 Arrive back at Liberty Park at 900 South. Cool off in the park's pool or splash in the fountains at the kids' playground.

15 Bonneville Shoreline Trail (Parleys Crossing)

This section of the Bonneville Shoreline Trail (BST) breaks from the traditional dirt trails and follows paved residential streets through charming east-side neighborhoods. The Parleys Crossing section over Interstate 80 at the mouth of Parleys Canyon was the crucial link if the BST had any hopes of being a continuous route along the Wasatch Range's foothills. Whether ridden as a commuter route or as a quick morning or evening spin, the BST showcases the local commitment to the regional trail system and shows off the beauty of the Wasatch Front.

Start: Sunnyside Avenue trailhead at mouth of Emigration Canyon.
Distance: 8.4 miles out-and-back.
Gain: 560 feet.
Physical difficulty: Easy. A large portion of the trail is nearly flat, but there are two very steep climbs on the Parleys Crossing section, one in each direction and each at about 9 percent grade. Fortunately, the climbs are little more than a couple hundred yards long. If your bike has a triple chainring, then the climbs should be a piece of cake. If your bike sports race gearing, then you'll have to pump hard but only briefly. The rest is a breeze.
Margin of comfort: Fair to good. Most of the route follows residential roads that have no shoulders, but traffic is light and the speed limit is low. These roads are signed as the designated route of the BST, although there are no bike lanes. The Parleys Crossing section is a 10-foot-wide, two-lane, paved, nonmotorized trail.
Season: March through November or whenever it is snow free and you can brave the cold.
Maps: USGS 1:24,000: Fort Douglas and Sugarhouse, Utah.

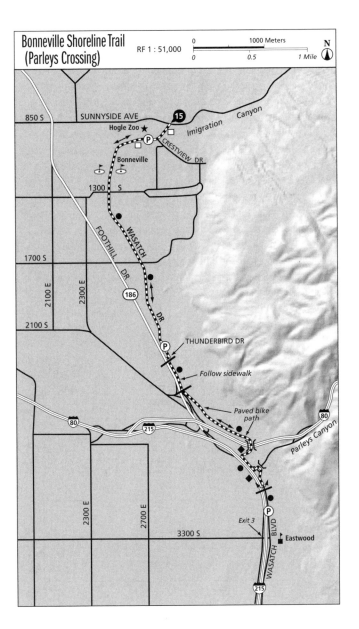

Bonneville Shoreline Trail
(Parleys Crossing)

RF 1 : 51,000

0   1000 Meters
0   0.5   1 Mile

N

850 S   SUNNYSIDE AVE

15

Imigration Canyon

Hogle Zoo ★

P

CRESTVIEW DR

Bonneville

1300 S

WASATCH

1700 S

FOOTHILL DR

186

2100 E

2300 E

2100 S

P   THUNDERBIRD DR

Follow sidewalk

Paved bike path

80

215

80

Parleys Canyon

2300 E

2700 E

3300 S

Exit 3

P

WASATCH BLVD

■ Eastwood

215

Finding the trailhead: From the intersection of Foothill Drive (1950 East) and Sunnyside Avenue (850 South), take Sunnyside east 1 mile and park at the trailhead for the BST, which is just east of Hogle Zoo and opposite Crestview Drive. Or park at nearby Rotary Glen Park. Alternatively, you could ride south to north from the Wasatch Boulevard Trailhead. From the intersection of 3300 South and Wasatch Boulevard (3565 East), go north on Wasatch for 0.5 mile to the parking area at the road's end. (Southbound on Interstate 215, take exit 3 for 3300 South. Northbound on I-215, take exit 4 for 3300 South/3900 South.)

Know before you go: The Parleys Crossing section has steep grades and sharp turns on a 10-foot-wide, two-way, paved bike lane; ride cautiously and be alert to other trail users. This is not a race course. Watch out for pylons in the middle of the path on both sides of the two bridges on the Parleys Crossing section. You must share the road with vehicles elsewhere. Ride cautiously on Wasatch Drive because not all intersections are four-way stops.

The Ride

Here's the ride going from north to south.

0.0 From the BST trailhead at the intersection of Sunnyside Avenue and Crestview Drive, cross Sunnyside and climb Crestview. It's steep but it's only a few hundred yards long.

0.2 Turn right atop the hill onto Wasatch Drive and coast past Bonneville Golf Course.

0.9 Cross 1300 South and ride through the neighborhood.

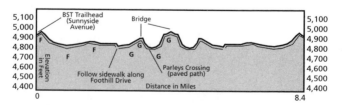

2.0 Veer left at the Y-intersection with Broadmoor Drive, following BST and bike route signs along Wasatch Drive.

2.5 Turn right at the T-junction with Thunderbird Drive. At the stoplight at Foothill Drive, hop onto the wide sidewalk on the road's east side. The sidewalk is posted as the official route of the BST, so there is no need to ride on busy Foothill Drive.

2.8 Join with the paved bike path for the Parleys Crossing section of the BST. Mount Olympus's slabby quartzite breast-plates tower over the Salt Lake Valley and are square in your sights. You can look across the entire Salt Lake Valley from Point of the Mountain in the south to Ensign Peak in the north. The path curves into the mouth of Parleys Canyon right above I-80.

3.3 Cross the north bridge over I-80, descend quickly, and slow down for the hairpin left turn. The path follows I-215 and passes Suicide Rock, which has been the longtime target for those with spray paint or a brush. Gear down and spin or stand and pump hard for the 9-percent hill rising up on the south side.

4.1 Cross the south bridge over the highway.

4.2 Exit to the parking area at the end of Wasatch Boulevard. Again, Mount Olympus is straight ahead. This is the turn-around point.

8.4 Arrive back at the Sunnyside Avenue trailhead.

16 Josie Johnson Memorial Ride

Bicyclists of all ages, interests, and abilities unite annually to ride in remembrance of cyclists who were killed in car collisions on Utah's roads and to raise awareness for bicycle safety. Josie Johnson, after whom the ride was founded, was killed on September 18, 2004, while riding in Big Cottonwood Canyon. In 2005 the ride attracted more than 1,000 bicyclists and was led by hometown pro rider and 2005 Tour de France stage winner Dave Zabriskie. Although Dave won the Prologue time trial, the pace on the memorial ride is kept casual.

Also known as the Cotton Bottom Loop, this ride is a local favorite on which you'll find sponsor-clad racers and recreational riders alike. Starting at Sugarhouse Park, the first half of the loop wanders through east-side neighborhoods and small business districts. The second half follows Wasatch Boulevard from Big Cottonwood Canyon to the paved Bonneville Shoreline Trail at Parleys Canyon. The loop finishes with another short tour through neighborhoods back to Sugarhouse Park. Although some roads have moderate traffic, the entire loop follows roads that have built-in bike lanes or are designated bike routes.

Start: Park at Sugarhouse Park and begin the ride at Highland High School.
Distance: 20.2-mile loop.
Gain: 1,000 feet.
Physical difficulty: Moderate. This is a great endurance ride because there are lots of flat stretches to spin at high cadence plus a few rolling hills to pump up your heart, but there are no significant hills to grind your quads.
Margin of comfort: Good. The route follows roads that are

designated bike routes with 3-foot-wide shoulders. Several roads, including Wasatch Boulevard, have bike lanes.

Season: March through November and throughout winter when the roads are dry and you can brave the cold.

Maps: USGS 1:24,000: Draper and Sugarhouse Park, Utah.

Finding the trailhead: The Josie Johnson Memorial Ride officially begins at Sugarhouse Park (1500 East and 2100 South). For the sake of simplicity, the ride log below begins at the intersection of 1700 East and 2100 South at Highland High School.

Know before you go: Some roads receive moderate traffic, so be aware of motorists. Naturally, you can log into this ride anywhere along its length. See the options below for shortening the loop.

The Ride

- **0.0** From the intersection of 1700 East and 2100 South at Highland High School, head south on 1700 East (bike lane).
- **0.7** Take the second left after crossing the bridge over Interstate 80 onto Stratford Avenue and pedal up a slight grade through the neighborhood. (If you miss the turn, then simply go left at the T-intersection with 2700 South.)
- **1.2** Turn right onto 2000 East (bike route).
- **1.3** Cross 2700 South (or turn right onto 2000 East if you came up 2700 South instead of Stratford).
- **2.2** Cross 3300 South after a mile-long straightaway flat. The shoulder pinches to less than 1 foot temporarily.
- **2.4** Pass Evergreen Middle School and cross Evergreen Avenue (3455 South).
- **2.8** Go through an X-intersection and four-way stop to continue south on 2000 East.
- **3.8** Turn right at a four-way stop onto Terra Linda Drive, then take the first left onto Albright Drive.

4.2 Cross 4500 South to continue south on what is now Holladay Boulevard (bike route). **Bail-out:** Short on time? Instead of making the full loop down to the Cotton Bottom Inn and up to 1700 South, try this short course. You'll knock it off in a little over a half hour. After zigzagging on Terra Linda and Albright to 4500 South, go left/east on 4500 South and climb gradually to 2700 East. Go left/north on 2700 East, angle around the S-turn on Hillside Lane, and take Evergreen Avenue back to 2000 East. Retrace your tracks to Sugarhouse Park. Total distance is about 10 miles.

4.7 2300 East merges from the left at a stoplight; then cross Murray-Holladay Boulevard at a stoplight (business district). Use caution at this intersection and watch for turning cars.

5.7 Continue south on a near level keel and pass Cottonwood Elementary School. By now you will have left the business district and will enjoy a magnificent view of Mount Olympus.

7.0 Cross 6200 South, pass the Cotton Bottom Inn (famous for their garlic burgers), and follow the bike route signs.

7.3 Pass under Interstate 215 and turn left onto the paved Old Mill Trail, which crosses a footbridge over Big Cottonwood Creek. (The road ahead ends at a parking garage.) Veer right, following the signed bike route through the parking lots for Old Mill Corporate Center III.

7.5 Exit the business center next to Foothill Family Clinic and cross 3000 East at the stoplight. Continue on Big Cottonwood Canyon Road/6485 South (bike route). The road rises slightly and follows the creek's riparian bank.

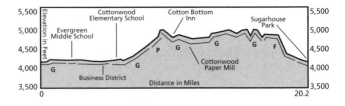

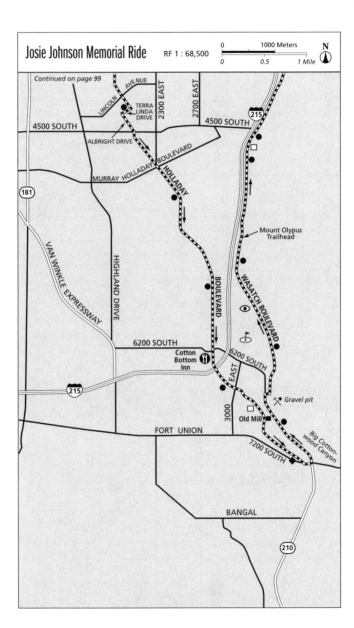

Josie Johnson Memorial Ride

RF 1 : 68,500

0   1000 Meters
0   0.5   1 Mile

N

Continued on page 99

LINCOLN AVENUE

TERRA LINDA DRIVE

ALBRIGHT DRIVE

2300 EAST

2700 EAST

4500 SOUTH

4500 SOUTH

215

MURRAY HOLLADAY BOULEVARD

HOLLADAY

181

VAN WINKLE EXPRESSWAY

HIGHLAND DRIVE

BOULEVARD

WASATCH BOULEVARD

Mount Olypus Trailhead

6200 SOUTH

Cotton Bottom Inn

6200 SOUTH

215

3000 EAST

Gravel pit

Old Mill

Big Cotton-wood Canyon

FORT UNION

7200 SOUTH

BANGAL

210

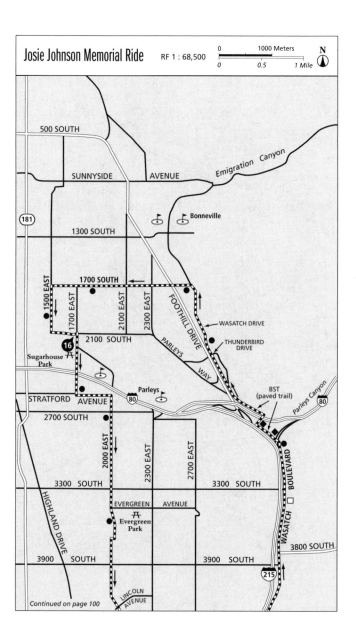

Josie Johnson Memorial Ride

RF 1 : 68,500

500 SOUTH

SUNNYSIDE AVENUE

Emigration Canyon

(181)

1300 SOUTH

Bonneville

1700 SOUTH

1500 EAST

1700 EAST

2100 EAST

2300 EAST

FOOTHILL DRIVE

WASATCH DRIVE

2100 SOUTH

PARLEYS WAY

THUNDERBIRD DRIVE

16

Sugarhouse Park

STRATFORD AVENUE

Parleys

BST (paved trail)

Parleys Canyon

80

2700 SOUTH

2000 EAST

2300 EAST

2700 EAST

WASATCH BOULEVARD

3300 SOUTH

3300 SOUTH

HIGHLAND DRIVE

EVERGREEN AVENUE

Evergreen Park

3800 SOUTH

3900 SOUTH

3900 SOUTH

215

Continued on page 100

LINCOLN AVENUE

8.1 Pass the historic Cottonwood Paper Mill.

8.9 Pump up a short, steep hill and turn left onto Fort Union Boulevard/7200 South. (This is probably the toughest hill on the route, and it barely rates as a "hill.")

9.0 Turn left onto Wasatch Boulevard (bike route) at the mouth of Big Cottonwood Canyon. Use caution crossing traffic into the left-turn lane, and be aware of traffic merging onto Wasatch after you make the turn. Rev it up on the slight downhill. Watch out for debris in the road and for turning trucks when you pass the gravel pit.

10.0 Turn right at the stoplight to continue on Wasatch Boulevard, which now has a bike lane. (6200 South goes straight and returns to Holladay Boulevard at the Cotton Bottom Inn if you want to retrace your tracks.) A long flat stretch curves around the base of the central Wasatch Range and affords a panoramic view of the entire Salt Lake Valley.

13.2 Cross 4500 South. **Bail-out:** Need a shortcut back to Sugarhouse Park? If so, take 4500 South downhill from Wasatch Boulevard and turn right onto 2700 East. Go around the S-turn on Hillside Lane (about 3500 South) and fork left onto Evergreen Avenue. Cross 2300 East, pass Evergreen Park (alternate trailhead), and turn right onto 2000 East to close the loop. Retrace your tracks to Sugarhouse Park. Total distance is 19 miles.

15.0 Go right at the stoplight at 3300 South, then veer left immediately to continue Wasatch Boulevard (3565 East).

15.5 Hop onto the paved Bonneville Shoreline Trail where the road ends at a parking lot. Heed the cautionary signs warning of steep grades and sharp turns on the path. Cross Parleys Canyon near Suicide Rock and grind up a steep hill to the bridge over I-80. Glance over your left shoulder at the majestic sight of Mount Olympus. Follow the wide sidewalk along Foothill Drive (bike route) after the path ends.

17.2 Turn right onto Thunderbird Drive, then immediately left onto Wasatch Drive (different than Wasatch Boulevard), and cruise through the Foothills neighborhood.

18.0 Turn left onto 1700 South and descend quickly to Foothill Drive.

18.3 Cross Foothill Drive at the stoplight. Go straight through the stoplights at 2300 East and 2100 East, both of which have bike lanes if you need to access the loop from other locations.

19.4 Cross 1700 East. If you didn't park at Sugarhouse Park, or if you joined the loop elsewhere, then go left onto 1700 East (bike lane) to return to the ride's start point at the intersection of 2100 South and 1700 East. If you need to reenter Sugarhouse Park, then it's best to continue.

19.7 Turn left onto 1500 East (bike lane).

20.2 Cross 2100 South and arrive at Sugarhouse Park.

17 Wasatch Boulevard

This is a classic ride that traces the foothills of its namesake mountains. Gently rolling terrain and long flat stretches are kind to the legs of novice riders, and they make a perfect time trial course for racers-in-training. The views gained throughout the ride capture the essence of the metro-to-mountains transition of northern Utah. Two short, stiff climbs will call upon your power reserves, but the rest of the route is all about high-cadence spinning. You can tap into this ride from anywhere along its route, or it can be added on to the Dimple Dell Loop out of Draper or Sandy for an even longer haul.

Start: Bonneville Shoreline Trailhead at about 3000 South and Wasatch Boulevard (3565 East).
Distance: 21.8-mile lariat-shaped loop.
Gain: 1,300 feet.
Physical difficulty: Moderate. Lots of flat stretches and gently rolling hills. There are two short, sharp climbs: south of Big Cottonwood Canyon and past La Caille Restaurant up to Little Cottonwood Canyon Road.
Margin of comfort: Fair to good overall. From 3300 South to 6200 South, Wasatch Boulevard has a bike lane. Over the rest of the road, the shoulder is generally 3 feet or more; *however,* it is less than 1 foot on the half-mile climb south of Big Cottonwood Canyon and traffic can be heavy. This section of road is a tight squeeze and warrants caution. The shoulder is less than 1 foot on Little Cottonwood Canyon Road/9800 South also, but traffic is generally light.
Season: March through November and throughout winter whenever the road is dry and you can brave the cold.
Maps: USGS 1:24,000: Draper and Sugarhouse, Utah.

Finding the trailhead: If you are southbound on Interstate 215, take exit 3 for 3300 South. If you are northbound on I-215, take exit 4 for 3900 South/3300 South. From the intersection of 3300 South and Wasatch Boulevard, go east, then bend immediately north (Wasatch Boulevard becomes 3565 East). The road ends in a half mile at the parking area for the Bonneville Shoreline Trail.

Other parking areas are at Upper Mill Creek Park on Wasatch Boulevard just north of 3800 South, the park-and-ride lot at Wasatch Boulevard and 3900 South, the park-and-ride lot at Big Cottonwood Canyon, the park-and-ride lot at Wasatch Boulevard and 3500 East/8165 South, and at Temple Quarry Nature Trail at Little Cottonwood Canyon. Naturally, you can start this ride anywhere along the route.

Know before you go: Traffic is heaviest between 3300 South and 4500 South and between 6200 South and the La Caille turnoff. Be cautious riding up the hill south of Big Cottonwood Canyon (past the racquet club) because the shoulder is less than 1 foot and traffic can be heavy. Stay in single file and as far right as possible. The wind typically blows out of the south, especially a day or two in advance of a storm front. If so, you'll reach speeds of a pro peloton on the northbound leg.

The Ride

0.0 Starting at the parking lot at the end of Wasatch Boulevard/3565 East, pedal south and enjoy a whopping view of Mount Olympus dead in your sights.

0.5 Go left at the intersection with 3300 South. Pick up the bike lane along Wasatch. I-215 is just below you.

1.4 Cross 3900 South (the park-and-ride lot is on the northwest corner). Pass Olympus Hills Shopping Center. Enjoy a good view across the Salt Lake Valley to the Oquirrh Mountains as you make your way past Mount Olympus. The massive tailing piles of the Kennecott's Bingham Canyon Copper Mine are clearly visible on the Oquirrhs.

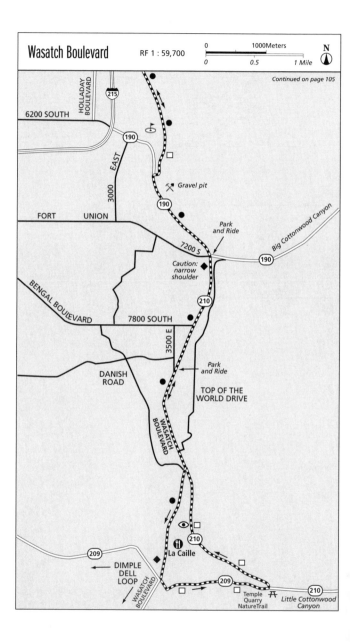

Wasatch Boulevard

RF 1 : 59,700

Continued on page 105

N

HOLLADAY BOULEVARD

6200 SOUTH

215

190

3000   EAST

Gravel pit

190

FORT   UNION

7200 S

Park and Ride

Big Cottonwood Canyon

190

Caution: narrow shoulder

210

BENGAL BOULEVARD

7800 SOUTH

3500 E

DANISH ROAD

Park and Ride

TOP OF THE WORLD DRIVE

WASATCH BOULEVARD

209

DIMPLE DELL LOOP

WASATCH BOULEVARD

210

La Caille

210

209

Temple Quarry NatureTrail

Little Cottonwood Canyon

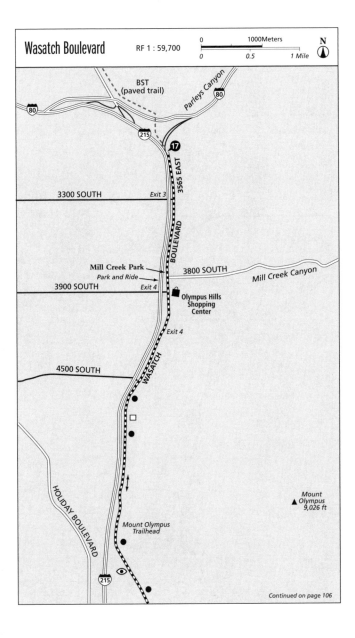

Wasatch Boulevard

RF 1 : 59,700

BST (paved trail)

Parleys Canyon

3300 SOUTH — Exit 3

3565 EAST

BOULEVARD

Mill Creek Park

Park and Ride

3800 SOUTH

Mill Creek Canyon

3900 SOUTH — Exit 4

Olympus Hills Shopping Center

Exit 4

WASATCH

4500 SOUTH

WASATCH

HOLIDAY BOULEVARD

Mount Olympus Trailhead

Mount Olympus 9,026 ft

Continued on page 106

2.4 Cross 4500 South and descend slightly. A half mile of sound barrier walls block your view of the valley but also deaden the buzz of traffic on I-215 below.

4.0 Pass the Mount Olympus Trailhead. The road curves slightly, and Lone Peak on the distant Alpine Ridge comes straight into view. Twin Peaks on the Cottonwood Ridge tower overhead in the middle ground. On the back/south side of Mount Olympus, Heughs Canyon is lined with blocky cliffs of brown quartzites.

5.6 Come to the intersection with 6200 South/Highway 190. Turn left to continue on Wasatch Boulevard/Highway 190, which widens to four lanes. Be watchful of gravel and debris on the shoulder. Traffic can be fast and heavy.

6.6 Go through the intersection with Fort Union Boulevard/7200 South (right) and Big Cottonwood Canyon Road/Highway 190 (left). Gear down for one of the route's steepest climbs. As you pass the Canyon Racquet Club, the shoulder narrows to less than 1 foot, and traffic can be heavy and fast. Ride cautiously and hold your line.

8.9 Fork right to continue on Wasatch Boulevard toward La Caille to begin the loop portion of the route counterclockwise, or go straight and ride the loop clockwise. Both ways have a steep climb, and neither direction is harder than the other. The climb past La Caille (counterclockwise), described here, is shorter but is followed by a steady, gentle grade on Little Cottonwood Canyon Road/9800 South. Going straight (clockwise), the hill is longer, but then you're done. It's your choice.

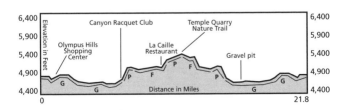

9.7 Pass the entrance to La Caille Restaurant and chug uphill.

10.1 Turn left onto Little Cottonwood Canyon Road (9800 South/Highway 209). The shoulder is less than 1 foot. Climb gradually.

10.2 Pass the parking area/trailhead for the Lower Bells Canyon Reservoir Trail/Bonneville Shoreline Trail. The road rises gradually into the mouth of Little Cottonwood Canyon and affords a long view straight up the glacial valley to the peaks of Snowbird and Alta.

11.3 Go left on Highway 210 and exit the canyon. To learn about the area's early history, take a stroll around the Temple Quarry Nature Trail. Those with a penchant for geology will notice the contact unconformity between the older dark brown quartzites and the younger light gray monzanite (a type of granite) that intruded on them from below.

12.4 Crest the hill and take in the exceptional view of the Salt Lake Valley all the way north to Salt Lake City's central business district. Tuck-and-glide down the hill, but be ready to slam on the brakes at the bottom if the light turns red.

13.0 Return to Wasatch Boulevard at the La Caille junction to close the loop, and retrace your tracks northward.

16.2 Pass the gravel pit (watch for gravel in the road and for turning trucks) and turn right at the light to continue on Wasatch; 6200 South goes straight. Begin your time trial past Mount Olympus.

21.8 Arrive back at the parking area at the end of Wasatch Boulevard.

18 Emigration Canyon Road

Aptly named, Emigration Canyon was the final leg of the Mormon Pioneers' historic trek to the Salt Lake Valley in 1847, led by Brigham Young. Today the canyon's paved road is one of the most popular rides in the Wasatch Range. With ride-to access from the city's "foothills," gentle to moderate grades, light to moderate traffic, and two quaint cafes (Ruth's Diner and Sun and Moon Cafe), Emigration welcomes all riders. During late afternoon and on weekends, you'll find a steady stream of bicyclists, from racers in full regalia to rec riders in T-shirts, making their way up the canyon to Little Mountain Summit.

Start: Bonneville Shoreline Trail (BST) parking lot at the mouth of Emigration Canyon.

Distance: 15.6-mile out-and-back.

Gain: 1,270 feet.

Physical difficulty: Moderate. At an average 3 percent grade, Emigration Canyon is the easiest canyon ride in the Wasatch Range. Inasmuch, Emigration is a magnet for casual riders to racers-in-training. It's the perfect fitness ride, with long, consistently pitched, gentle grades broken by short inclines that demand slightly more effort. The last 1.8 miles steepens

to near 5 percent. If you wear a heart rate monitor, then you'll find Emigration makes for an ideal thirty-minute time trial.

Margin of comfort: Fair to good overall. It is poor for the first half mile at the canyon's mouth; good for the next 4 miles (bike lane), then fair to the Pinecrest turnoff; and good from Pinecrest to the summit. The bike lane is planned to be extended farther up the canyon in the future.

The shoulder varies from less than 1 foot for the first half mile to 4 feet for the majority of the climb.

Emigration Canyon Road

RF 1 : 72,500

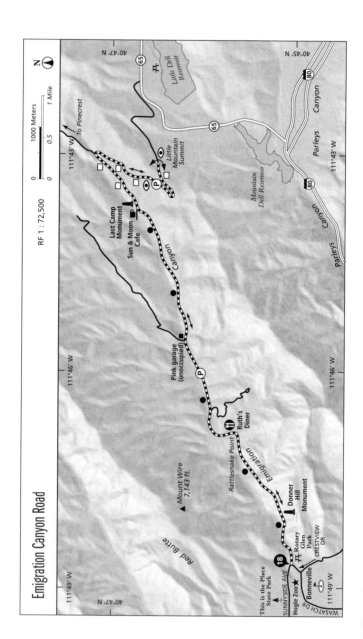

Season: March through November. Midday during midsummer is very warm.

Maps: USGS 1:24,000: Fort Douglas and Mountain Dell, Utah.

Finding the trailhead: From the intersection of Foothill Drive and Sunnyside Avenue (850 South), take Sunnyside east 1 mile and park at the trailhead for the BST, which is opposite Crestview Drive and just past Hogle Zoo. Or park at Rotary Glen Park across the road.

Know before you go: Traffic is mostly light, but can be moderate during evening rush hour and on weekends. The first half mile is narrow and curvy, the pavement is choppy, and the shoulder is less than 1 foot, so ride cautiously.

The Ride

0.0 From the BST parking lot, enter Emigration Canyon. Use caution here because the road is narrow and the shoulder is less than 1 foot. Donner Hill rises to your right, topped with condos and communication towers. In 1846, a year before the Mormons arrived in the Salt Lake Valley, the ill-fated Donner-Reed party labored over the small rocky knoll after toiling for sixteen days in northeastern Utah's canyons and mountains. These arduous delays proved fatal as the wagon train was later besieged by an early autumn blizzard in the Sierra Nevada, and members resorted to cannibalism to survive.

0.6 The bike lane begins, and the road rises gradually amidst rounded hills of oak and maple.

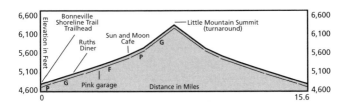

1.9 Pass Ruth's Diner, a popular lunch and weekend brunch stop.

2.4 This marks the end of the bike lane, at least for now. The bike lane will extend farther in years to come.

3.4 The old "pink garage" marks the turnoff for Emigration Oaks.

5.1 Pass Sun and Moon Cafe, then a historical marker for Brigham Young's last camp. This is where Brigham Young spent his last night before entering the Salt Lake Valley on July 24, 1847, and declaring it to be the right place for his Zion settlement.

5.7 The grade steepens slightly, and you'll shift down a gear or two.

6.0 The road switchbacks right at the turnoff for Pinecrest and steepens to about 5 percent. There are good views down the canyon and of the distant Oquirrh Mountains along this stretch. The original Mormon Pioneer Trail crosses the road.

7.7 You can see the summit. Get out of your saddle and sprint!

7.8 Crest Little Mountain Summit, the route's turnaround point. Little Dell Reservoir fills the canyon below, and the Mill Creek ridge hovers above distant Interstate 80. An interpretive plaque describes the exodus of the Mormon Pioneers from Nauvoo, Illinois, in 1846. Thousands of emigrants pulling and pushing heavy handcarts would follow in the coming years.

15.6 Arrive back at the BST parking lot.

19 East Canyon Road

Whether ridden by itself or tacked onto either the Parleys Canyon/I–80 ride or Emigration Canyon Road, the East Canyon Road to Big Mountain Pass has a Euro feel, as the last several miles switchback steeply to the 7,420-foot-high "col." It's hardly *hors de categorie*, but it's a stiff climb just the same. Racers might dance on their pedals up the grade; mortals will be wishing for lower gears.

Those not hell-bent on dropping the peloton will be interested to know that the ride has historical significance, as it was the chosen route of the Mormon Pioneers, California Trail, Pony Express, Overland Stage, and original telegraph line between 1846 and 1861.

Start: East Canyon Road by Mountain Dell Golf Course, 5 miles east of Salt Lake City.
Distance: 16.2-mile out-and-back.
Gain: 1,880 feet.
Physical difficulty: Moderately strenuous. The ride starts with a 1.5-mile climb at 6 percent grade that will jump-start your heart faster than a double shot of espresso. A long, gradual approach precedes the final 3-mile, 7 percent grind to Big Mountain Pass. The return flight is a huge return on your climbing investment.

Margin of comfort: Fair overall. It is good for the first 3 miles and fair for the remainder, as the shoulder is less than 1 foot but traffic is generally light (might be moderate on weekends and holidays). The road is signed SHARE THE ROAD throughout.
Season: April to November, depending on when the seasonal road closure gate is open. The final climb to the pass is a scorcher at midday during midsummer, when temperatures can exceed 90 degrees.
Maps: USGS 1:24,000: Mountain Dell, Utah.

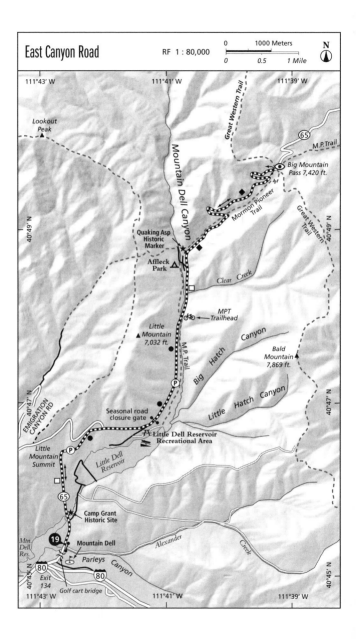

East Canyon Road

RF 1 : 80,000

0   1000 Meters

0   0.5   1 Mile

N

111°43' W   111°41' W   111°39' W

Lookout
Peak ▲

Great Western Trail

65
M.P. Trail

Big Mountain
Pass 7,420 ft.

Mountain Dell Canyon

Mormon Pioneer Trail

Great Western Trail

40°49' N

Quaking Asp
Historic Marker

Affleck
Park

Clear Creek

40°49' N

MPT
Trailhead

Little
Mountain ▲
7,032 ft.

M.P. Trail

Big Hatch Canyon

Bald
Mountain ▲
7,869 ft.

40°47' N

P

Little Hatch Canyon

Seasonal road
closure gate

Little Dell Reservoir
Recreational Area

EMIGRATION CANYON RD

40°47' N

Little
Mountain
Summit

P

Little Dell Reservoir

65

Camp Grant
Historic Site

Mtn.
Dell
Res.

19

Mountain Dell

Alexander   Creek

40°45' N

80

Parleys Canyon

80

Exit
134

Golf cart bridge

111°43' W   111°41' W   111°39' W

40°45' N

Finding the trailhead: From Salt Lake City drive (or pedal) 5 miles up Interstate 80 in Parleys Canyon and take exit 134 for East Canyon and Highway 65. Go left on Highway 65 for 0.3 mile, pass under the golf cart bridge for Mountain Dell Golf Course, and park roadside near a brown gate posted AUTHORIZED VEHICLES ONLY.

Know before you go: Traffic on East Canyon Road/Highway 65 is generally light but might be moderate on weekends with lumbering RVs and trucks towing boats to East Canyon Reservoir. Be aware of vehicles approaching from behind. Use caution when descending because the switchbacks are tight and there might be fallen rocks in the road. Also, be leery of motorists shortcutting the switchbacks.

The Ride

0.0   Park and embark from near the brown gate just north of the golf cart bridge for Mountain Dell Golf Course.

0.4   Your legs will warm up quickly on the 1.5-mile-long 6 percent grade. Looking left, you'll see Mountain Dell Reservoir. On the right you'll pass a historical marker noting that the Donner-Reed party camped here in August 1846 while cutting a wagon road over Little Mountain Summit and into Emigration Canyon. The following year the site was named Camp Grant for Jedediah Grant, a Mormon Pioneer and Salt Lake City's first mayor.

2.0   Pass the turnoff for Emigration Canyon. Stay straight on Highway 65 for East Canyon.

2.6   Pass the entrance to Little Dell Reservoir Recreation Area. There is an outhouse near the road but no water tap.

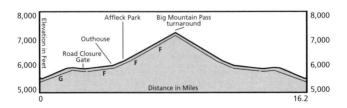

2.8 Pass the seasonal road closure gate. The road rises gradually, and the shoulder is less than 1 foot. Mountain Dell Canyon is bound by tall rounded summits covered with brushy oak and maple, and the lush fields below are known to lure moose and other big game. (Contrary to the road's name, you are riding up Mountain Dell Canyon. The road is named for the canyon and reservoir on the other side of the pass.)

4.3 Pass the trailhead for the Mormon Pioneer Trail. There is an outhouse but no water tap.

5.0 Pass the entrance to Affleck Park. The grade steepens.

5.2 The grade locks in at 7 percent, and you'll be compelled to summon your lowest gears. The canyon splits and the highway goes up the right fork beneath ruddy cliffs of blocky conglomerate. You can see the road cuts above, and you get a quick glimpse of your destination—the communication towers atop Big Mountain Pass about 3 miles away.

6.0 The road switchbacks left and you cross the Mormon Pioneer Trail, marked ORIGINAL TRAIL. (See the Mormon Pioneer Trail ride.) You rise quickly above the canyon and can sight south to peaks on the Mill Creek Canyon ridge.

6.4 The road switchbacks right—steeply. Aspens populate hollows creasing the canyon's slopes, and the Mormon Pioneer Trail can be seen etched into the hillside.

8.1 Sprint to the county line at Big Mountain Pass. Pull into the gravel parking area (outhouse but no water tap) and read the interpretive plaque commemorating the trek of the Mormon Pioneers and others who traveled the route of your bike ride between 1846 and 1861. Can you imagine hauling a 500-pound handcart over the pass without any road to follow? The Mormon Pioneer Trail crosses the pass and descends Little Emigration Canyon to East Canyon Creek. The Great Western Trail also crosses the pass on its 3,000-mile journey from Canada to Mexico. Enjoy the scenic view south of Mount Aire and Grandeur Peak on the Mill Creek Canyon ridge and of the distant Salt Lake Valley. You can even make out the colossal mine tailings of Kennecott's Bingham Canyon Copper Mine on the faraway Oquirrh Mountains. This is the turnaround point. The return descent is a large part of the reason why you made this climb. Rounding the tight switchbacks is thrilling, and you can reach highway speeds on the straightaways if you tuck-and-glide (with a favorable wind).

16.2 Arrive back at the gate north of the golf cart bridge.

20 **Parleys Canyon/I-80**

Despite Interstate 80 being a major transportation corridor between Salt Lake City and all points east, Parleys Canyon is quite popular with bicyclists. Named after Parley Pratt, a Mormon Pioneer who first built a toll road up the canyon to Park City in the mid-1800s, Parleys Canyon mixes gentle and steep grades where you can perfect your high-cadence "tempo" riding or build raw climbing power. Granted, the constant whir of vehicles whizzing by is a nuisance, but you'll get numb to it. Endurance junkies can use Parleys as a stepping-stone for longer treks to Park City or up East Canyon Road.

Start: The I-80/Interstate 215 interchange at the mouth of Parleys Canyon.
Distance: 22-mile out-and-back.
Gain: 2,300 feet.
Physical difficulty: Moderately strenuous. Riders with modest fitness and reasonably low gearing will find the climb to be a sit-and-spin "tempo" ride. If your bike lacks low gears, then you'll be pumping hard at low cadence most of the way. Although truckers are warned of the canyon's 3 to 6 percent grades, your brakes won't be smoking on the return descent, as it requires a fair amount of pedaling.
Margin of comfort: Fair. Getting into Parleys Canyon can be

Parleys Canyon/I-80; Mill Creek Canyon Road

RF 1 : 116,300

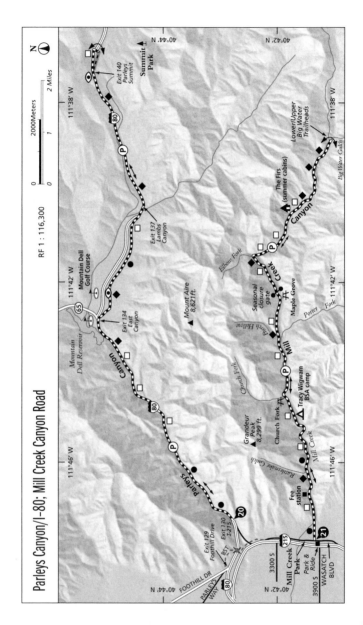

unnerving because the shoulder on the on ramps can be less than 3 feet, and you might have to cross merging traffic. Once in the canyon, the shoulder is 8 feet or more, but high-speed traffic is heavy. A rumble strip next to the white line forces you far to the right where there might be roadside debris.

Season: March through October. When inversions hit the valley during midwinter, you'll find sunny skies and pleasant climes in the canyon above Mountain Dell Reservoir.

Maps: USGS 1:24,000: Big Dutch Hollow, Fort Douglas, Mount Aire, Mountain Dell, Park City West, and Sugarhouse, Utah.

Finding the trailhead: From the south hop onto I–215 at the intersection of 3300 South and Wasatch Boulevard. Take exit 2 for I–80 east (Park City, Cheyenne). From the north ride on Foothill Drive and then take the cloverleaf entrance ramp onto I–80 (Park City, Cheyenne). From the west pedal up Parleys Way (2100 South), merge with Foothill Drive, and immediately take the cloverleaf entrance ramp onto I–80 (Park City, Cheyenne).

Know before you go: Bicycle travel is legal on this stretch of interstate highway because it provides the only transportation corridor between Salt Lake and Park City. Inasmuch, be forewarned that you'll brush shoulders with fast-moving vehicles and trucks. Stay to the far right side of the shoulder and ride in single file. Beware of roadside debris and gravel on the shoulder. Puncture-resistant tires are recommended. Use *extreme* caution entering I–80 from the north and west because you must cross traffic lanes on entrance ramps. Likewise, use caution and be aware of traffic behind you farther up the canyon when you must cross traffic lanes at exit ramps. A prevalent up-canyon wind is a boon to climbing, but it's a bane to descending, and you might have to pedal hard down the lower canyon.

To exit Parleys Canyon: Northbound bicyclists take exit 129 for Foothill Drive. Westbound bicyclists take exit 129 for Foothill Drive, then veer left onto Parleys Way before reaching Foothill. Parleys Way feeds into 2100 South. Southbound riders are advised to not take exit

130 for I-215 because the curves and narrow shoulder make for a very poor margin of comfort. Instead, follow the route for northbound bicyclists by taking exit 129 for Foothill Drive. When you merge with Foothill, make a U-turn to the right and onto the paved Bonneville Shoreline Trail (BST), which is bridged over I-80. The BST exits to the end of Wasatch Boulevard, which leads to its intersection with 3300 South. Regardless of your route out of Parleys, wait for traffic to clear behind you before crossing any exit lanes. Bikes are not allowed on I-80 west of Parleys Canyon; therefore, you *must* take exit 129.

The Ride

0.0 So that all bicyclists are on the same page, regardless of their approach to Parleys Canyon, the ride begins where exit 2 from I-215 north merges with I-80 heading up Parleys Canyon. Start out by enjoying gentle 2 to 3 percent grades for several miles. Here Parleys Canyon is bound by tall barren hills covered with patches of tenacious oak.

1.7 Pass exit 131 for the gun range. There are no services, but you have a chance to turn around.

3.2 Pass exit 132 (ranch access). There are no services, but you have a chance to turn around.

4.0 Pass exit 133 (utility exit). There are no services, but you have a chance to turn around. Just beyond, the grade steepens to 6 percent as you approach exit 134 for East Canyon. Gear down.

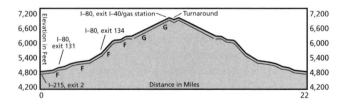

5.0 The grade steepens to 7 percent as you pass exit 134 for East Canyon and Highway 65. (See the East Canyon Road ride.) Beyond the exit ramp you have a good view north of Mountain Dell Golf Course and of the rolling highlands above Emigration and Mountain Dell Canyons.

7.5 Pass exit 137 for Lambs Canyon. Now the highway tilts up to 6 percent grade and remains there until Parleys Summit. Loaded semis get overburdened on this stretch, and if you have the fast-twitch legs of a sprinter, you can drag-race the slower-moving ones until your quads blow. The canyon's brushy slopes now hint of alpine elevations by supporting groves of aspen and fir.

10.4 Take exit 140 for Parleys Summit. To turn around you must first descend the exit ramp. You can refuel at the gas station or No Worries Cafe to the right of the exit ramp.

11.0 To turn around cross under I–80, go left up the entrance ramp, and merge with I–80 at the brake test area. You should reach your ride's maximum speed if you tuck-and-glide down the six-percent grade coming off the summit. If you lift your head and squint through your teary eyes, then you'll find a fine view of Mount Aire dead in your sights. Past Lambs Canyon, you'll have to shift down and resume pedal-ing, but you'll tuck-and-glide again past exit 134 for East Canyon. The wind can howl up the lower canyon, and despite the 3 percent grade, you might have to shift to your small chainring to plod downhill.

22.0 Arrive back at the I–215/I–80 interchange.

21 Mill Creek Canyon Road

Although Mill Creek Canyon is the only central Wasatch canyon requiring a use fee (for motorists only), it is certainly one of the most popular summer destinations for car tourists, picnickers, anglers, hikers, and mountain bikers. The curvy road is a delight for road bikers, too. The road's stair-step rise—alternating steep and gentle grades—effectively breaks up the monotony of the climb and will keep your gears active. Over the first half of the ride, you'll salivate over the smoky aroma of dogs and burgers being grilled by picnickers; later on your lungs will fill with the sweet scent of pine. And all the while Mill Creek tumbles alongside the road, singing a dainty melody that encourages you to go on.

See map on page 118.

Start: Mill Creek Canyon entrance, at the intersection of 3800 South and Wasatch Boulevard.

Distance: 18.8-mile out-and-back.

Gain: 2,650 feet.

Physical difficulty: Strenuous. The canyon's many short, steep "micro hills" require brief but hard efforts, and the toll on your legs adds up quickly. In between these hills the canyon road is gentle to moderately pitched and a joy to spin up.

Margin of comfort: Fair. The shoulder is less than 1 foot up to Elbow Fork. From Elbow Fork to the top, there is no shoulder and the road narrows to just over one lane wide. Traffic is usually light during weekdays and moderate on weekends, and the speed limit is low. Motorists are generally alert and courteous to bicyclists.

Season: March through November in the lower canyon; May through October in the upper canyon.

Maps: USGS 1:24,000: Sugarhouse and Mount Aire, Utah.

Finding the trailhead: From Interstate 215 take exit 4 for 3900 South. Take Wasatch Boulevard 1 block north to 3800 South and turn right, following signs for Mill Creek Canyon. Obey signs restricting roadside parking. Good parking areas are the park-and-ride lot at the corner of 3900 South and Wasatch Boulevard or Upper Mill Creek Park just north of the 3800 South and Wasatch Boulevard intersection. There is limited parking near the canyon's fee station.

Know before you go: Mill Creek Canyon Road is popular with motorists, so ride in single file, stay to the far right side of the road, and use extra caution when descending because curves are blind and motorists might not be anticipating your approach.

Motorists are charged a fee upon exiting the canyon: $2.25. Bicyclists and pedestrians do not pay the fee. The seasonal road closure gate at Maple Grove Picnic Area is closed November 1 to June 30. During this time vehicles are prohibited in the upper canyon, except by special permit, but pedestrians and bicycles are allowed.

Picnic areas along the road and the Big Water Trailheads at the road's end have outhouses, but only Church Fork and Maple Grove Picnic Areas have water taps, which are usually turned on from Memorial Day to mid-September.

The Ride

0.0 From the intersection of Wasatch Boulevard and 3800 South, go through the four-way stop with Parkview Drive and enter the canyon. Warm up your legs on the gentle grade while eyeing the canyon's ledgy rock walls that are peppered with oak brush and junipers.

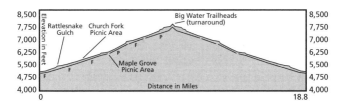

0.7 Pass the fee station.

1.2 The near 10 percent grade past the Wasatch-Cache National Forest sign will jump-start your heart; fortunately, it's no longer than what you can see, which is less than 0.2 mile. At midday during midsummer the sun beats down on your back relentlessly and your head might feel like it will self-combust.

1.5 Pass the Rattlesnake Gulch Trailhead for the Mill Creek Pipeline Trail. Welcome the respite as the road levels and is shaded by tall maples and cottonwoods. Mill Creek gushes alongside the road, and dunking your head seems all too inviting. From here on the road rises in stair-step fashion, where short, moderately strenuous hills are offset by gentle grades on which to recover.

3.1 Pass Church Fork Picnic Area and trailhead. Overhead, craggy hollows and chunky ridges wander through your view.

4.3 You'll summon your lowest gears as the road tilts upward briefly past the Burch Hollow Trailhead.

4.8 Pass Maple Grove Picnic Area and go through or around the seasonal closure gate. The grade increases slightly and holds remarkably steady for over a mile. Pick a cadence and pace yourself. Tall riparian growth drapes the road, and the shadows offer cool relief.

6.1 Ugh! The road rises sharply to over 10 percent for a couple hundred yards to Elbow Fork. This short, burly grind is a sample of things to come.

6.2 Bend right at Elbow Fork, which is the upper trailhead for the Mill Creek Pipeline Trail. This is a good turnaround point for those not wanting to go the distance. The road levels and aims south into the midday sun. Gradually the road narrows until it is little more than one-lane wide at times. Fir trees and aspens populate the slopes as the climate has cooled noticeably. Attack the numerous "micro hills" and then recover in between on gentler grades.

8.7 Dig deep for a short but burly two-stage hill about 0.1 mile long, recover quickly as you pass an overflow parking area, and punch it again up another steep shot into the conifers. The road narrows to one lane, so be aware of motorists.

9.3 Go full force up the protracted ramp to the Lower Big Water Trailhead.

9.4 Sprint to the Upper Big Water Trailhead and the road's end. Gravity takes hold quickly and firmly when descending. Be especially cautious between the top and Elbow Fork because the road is narrow and curves are tight and blind. The section between Elbow Fork and Maple Grove is blazing fast and potentially dangerous, especially when the gate at Maple Grove is closed. In addition, pedestrians and their pets (usually unleashed) can be all over the road, and they often seem oblivious to the fact that bicyclists are on the road, even though vehicles are prohibited. And you still might encounter motorists during the road closure season because some have special permits to The Firs summer cabin area. Athough bicyclists do not pay the fee upon exiting the canyon, you are required to stop at the fee station. Do not fly by at full throttle like Maverick did to the control tower in *Top Gun.*

18.8 Arrive back at 3800 South and Wasatch Boulevard.

22 Big Cottonwood Canyon Road

Big Cottonwood Canyon (BCC) is Salt Lake's classic test of endurance and climbing prowess, blending gradual spin-ups and leg-cramping inclines. Just making it up and down BCC garners due respect in the local cycling circle; knock it off with relative ease and you're ready for the race circuit. If you're a recreational rider and want to experience riding in a peloton, then sign up for the annual Big Cottonwood Hill Climb in July and test yourself against the region's best climbers.

Other than to peg your heart rate, ride BCC for its scenic beauty. The lower canyon is clutched by tall ragged walls of upended rock, whereas the upper canyon opens to glacier-cut bowls and treeless peaks. Interpretive signs along the way tell the story of the area's captivating geology and human history. To make your ride more complete, you can dine at a cafe, chat with rangers at a visitor center, or stroll a boardwalk around a placid pond.

Start: The intersection of Big Cottonwood Canyon Road and Wasatch Boulevard.
Distance: 29.4-mile out-and-back.
Gain: 3,850 feet.
Physical difficulty: Strenuous. The average grade is only 5 percent, but the law of averages can be misleading. Notorious climbs that gauge 8 percent or more are Storm Mountain, the Mill B S-curve, Silver Fork, and Solitude to Brighton. Surprisingly, there are several miles of gentle grades at the canyon's midsection.
Margin of comfort: Poor to fair. Although BCC is quite popular with cyclists and is posted SHARE THE ROAD, the road is a tight squeeze for vehicles and bikes as the shoulder is less than 1 foot the entire way. Motorists are generally alert and courteous to

bicyclists, but in 2004 a rider was hit and killed by a vehicle (see Josie Johnson Memorial Ride). Enough said.

Season: April through October.

Maps: USGS 1:24,000: Brighton, Draper, Dromedary Peak, Mount Aire, Park City West, and Sugarhouse, Utah.

Finding the trailhead: From Interstate 215 take exit 6 for 6200 South and the ski areas. Go east on 6200 South (Highway 190), then south on Wasatch Boulevard to the intersection of Fort Union Boulevard (7200 South) and Big Cottonwood Canyon Road. Start at the park-and-ride lot.

Know before you go: Riders should be physically fit and acclimated to high elevations for this ride. Be aware of traffic, ride in single file, stay to the far right, and ride defensively.

Food and drink are available at Silver Fork Lodge, Solitude Resort, and Brighton General Store. Water and restrooms are available at the Silver Lake Visitor Center at Brighton.

After midmorning the wind generally starts blowing up-canyon. This can ease the climb a bit, but it might turn the descent from a tuck-and-glide to steady pedaling.

The Ride

0.0 Start from the mouth of Big Cottonwood Canyon at Wasatch Boulevard. Immediately you pass a sign stating that you just crossed the Wasatch Fault. The initial gentle grade allows your legs to warm up gradually.

1.1 Pass Dogwood Picnic Area. The canyon's tall, ledgy, quartzite walls drop right down to the road's edge, and their near 90-degree tilt attests to the powerful tectonic forces that shaped the Wasatch Range.

2.1 The road angles up moderately as it passes the Stairs power plant. Your legs, heart, and lungs should be pumped up by now. Good thing, because they will be put to the test as the road bends right and arcs skyward for the steep, 0.8-mile pull up to Storm Mountain. This is one of the toughest

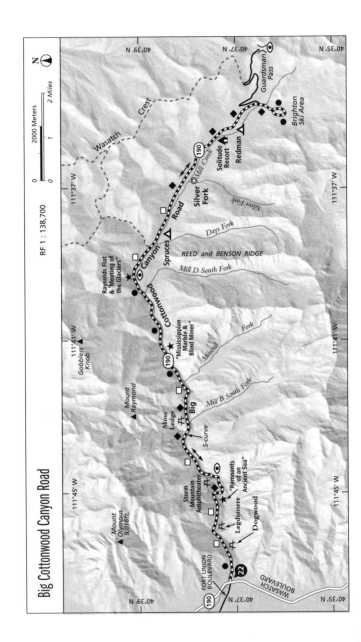

Big Cottonwood Canyon Road

RF 1 : 138,700

N

0   2000 Meters
0   1   2 Miles

Guardsman Pass

Brighton Ski Area

Solitude Resort

Redman

Silver Fork

Silver Fork

Days Fork

Mill Creek

REED and BENSON RIDGE

Mill D South Fork

Reynolds Flat & "Meeting of the Glaciers"

Canyon

Spruces

Cottonwood

Road

Wasatch

Crest

Gobblers Knob

Mount Raymond

"Mississippian Marble & Blind Miner"

Mineral

Fork

Moss Ledge

Big

S-curve

Mill B South Fork

Mount Olympus 9,016 ft.

Storm Mountain Amphitheater

"Remnants of an Ancient Sea"

Ledgemere

Dogwood

FORT UNION BOULEVARD

WASATCH BOULEVARD

190

22

190

40°39' N
40°37' N
40°35' N

111°45' W
111°41' W
111°37' W

climbs in the canyon at nearly 10 percent. An interpretive sign on the right tells of how the tilted purple and brown shales alongside the road are proof that northern Utah was once submerged beneath a shallow sea. Chalky smudge marks on the roadside cliffs are evidence that the area is popular with technical rock climbers, and you'll likely see them dangling from ropes through this section.

2.9 The road levels as it passes Storm Mountain Amphitheater and slips through tall road cuts. The road gets pinched here, so ride cautiously. The canyon's tilted strata form dramatic cliff faces and ragged couloirs that shuffle across your view like backdrops on a stage. A half mile farther the road rises moderately again.

4.4 The road rises steeply around the S-curve at the Mill B South Trailhead and for another half mile thereafter, requiring you to put full power to your pedal stroke.

5.2 Pass Moss Ledge Picnic Area and welcome gentle grades. If you are blessed with a tailwind, which is often the case, then you'll speed along. Did you ever think that climbing 4,000 vertical feet could be so easy here? One short stretch actually feels like you're going downhill. Enjoy the respite, but don't get used to it.

6.9 Spring water flows from a pipe on the north side of the road.

7.4 Pass the interpretive sign for MISSISSIPPIAN MARBLE, which describes how limestones were metamorphosed into chalky white marbles. A second plaque tells the story of the canyon's old mining town of Argenta and of a blind miner who prospected for ore despite his handicap.

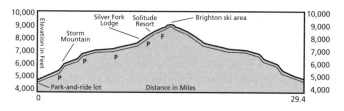

8.0   Pass another spring that gushes from the road cut. Fill your bottles and dunk your head; it's utterly refreshing.

9.0   Pass Reynolds Flat and the Mill D North Trailhead. The MEETING OF GLACIERS sign describes how an aggressive glacier coming out of Mill D South met the sluggish Big Cottonwood Canyon glacier, and how both stalled at this point. The lower canyon was thus stream cut, unlike Little Cottonwood Canyon, whose entire length was gouged by a glacier.

9.8   Climb moderately past Spruces Campground. Aspen and fir trees populate the canyon now and announce entry into the Canadian Life Zone.

11.3   The road tilts up steeply for the straightaway pull past Silver Fork Lodge and Restaurant. Dig deep, but pace yourself because the ride doesn't get much easier from here to the top.

12.4   Pass the Moonbeam Center entrance to Solitude Resort and welcome an all-too-quick respite.

12.8   Pass the main entrance to Solitude and resume climbing steeply past the resort's Tyrolean-style base facilities. The resort's Creekside Cafe calls out to you.

13.2   Pass Redman Campground. The road's continued steepness is relentless, and your legs will tell you that the ride is now one of attrition. The canyon widens, and crumbly, treeless peaks overshadow Solitude Resort and Brighton ski area. If you're not in your climbing groove, then you're suffering.

13.8   Recover quickly where the grade breaks at Camp Tuttle.

14.0   The Guardsman Pass Road forks left for Park City and Midway. Mark other riders in your group with a "Lance glance," and then punch it up the steep, 300-yard-long finale to the Brighton Loop Road. Ouch! If you're not in the fray, then you'll find the sights of Mounts Millicent, Tuscarora, and Wolverine to be marvelous. **Side-trip:** Guardsman Pass Road. You can add on 6 miles round-trip and another 1,100 vertical feet by climbing to Guardsman Pass. Views from the top of Big Cottonwood Canyon to the west and of Bonanza Flat and the Uinta Mountains to the east are worth the effort.

14.3 Go right on the loop road and pass Brighton Store and Cafe and the Silver Lake Visitor Center.

14.7 Pass the base of Brighton ski area and officially begin your well-earned downhill. The stretch from Brighton to Solitude and past Silver Fork is largely a tuck-and-glide, and you might exceed the 40 mph speed limit. Expect to pedal, in earnest if there's a headwind, between Spruces Campground and Moss Ledge Picnic Area; then square up for the high-speed stretch leading into the S curve at Mill B. Rounding the S curve with a full head of stream can be thrilling but also dangerous. Pedal and coast to Storm Mountain, then ready the brakes for the plummeting descent to the Stairs plant curve. Watch out for the left turn at the bottom; it comes on faster and sharper than you might think. The remaining descent is a pleasant spin.

29.4 Arrive back at the parking area.

23 Little Cottonwood Canyon Road

"Little" Cottonwood Canyon doesn't mean smaller or easier than Big Cottonwood Canyon. It means shorter and steeper. Unless you're using a triple chainring, there are few places to "spin" so climbing Little Cottonwood is all about putting power to the pedals. It's a climb that is well respected in the local cycling community, and those outside the spoked circle will just chuckle dumbfoundedly when you mention where you rode.

Riding up Little Cottonwood is more than a day of pain and suffering, although that's a large part of it. The sights of tall serrated ridges, lush valleys hanging above the glacially cut canyon, and snowfields clinging to cirques well into midsummer are truly inspirational. And you don't have to make a beeline back down either because there are always activities and good eats at Snowbird Resort and plenty of sightseeing at neighboring Alta.

Want a riding buddy? How about a few hundred? Then mark the annual Snowbird Hill Climb on your calendar. It's generally held in late August.

Start: The flashing billboard at the bottom Little Cottonwood Canyon.
Distance: 17.4-mile out-and-back.
Gain: 3,350 feet.
Physical difficulty: Extremely strenuous. Averaging a 7 percent grade, Little Cottonwood Canyon is the mother of hill climbs in Salt Lake. It packs a wallop from the start and keeps knocking you senseless to the top. Along the way you'll face many sections of 9 percent grade—and that's steep. Even the respites will have your heart redlined. Mortals will want a triple chainring, for sure.
Margin of comfort: Poor. Although the road is signed BIKE ROUTE, the shoulder is less than 1

foot and the two-lane road is narrow. Traffic is generally light, however, so motorists should be able to pass safely.

Season: April through October.
Maps: USGS 1:24,000: Draper, Dromedary Peak, and Brighton, Utah.

Finding the trailhead: From Interstate 215, take exit 6 for 6200 South and the ski areas. Travel east on 6200 South, then south on Wasatch Boulevard/Highway 190. Pass Big Cottonwood Canyon/Fort Union Boulevard and continue south on Highway 210, following signs for Alta and Snowbird. As you enter the canyon at the junction of Highway 210 and Highway 209, you can park at either the park-and-ride lot on the north side of the road or the Temple Quarry Nature Trail on the south side. The annual race starts at Alta Canyon Recreation Center at 9400 South and 2000 East.

Know Before You Go: Riders should be physically fit and acclimated to high elevations for this ride. Be aware of traffic, ride in single file, stay to the far right, and ride defensively. The descent is dangerously fast, so your brakes must be in perfect condition. Food and drink are available at Snowbird Resort and in the town of Alta.

A note about the descent: Obey the speed limit. Many sections are too steep and the curves are too sharp to ride without braking; do so prudently. Conversely, constant braking might superheat your rims and cause a blowout. Slow down when winding through the Seven Sisters turns to check out the view of the lower canyon as it enters the Salt Lake Valley. The U-shape canyon is a textbook example of alpine glaciation.

The Ride

0.0 Begin at the flashing billboard at the mouth of Little Cottonwood Canyon. Unlike Big Cottonwood Canyon, there's not much of a warm-up because Little Cottonwood Canyon Road tilts up moderately steeply from the start. Check out the long view up the canyon now because in short order your nose will be glued to the handlebar and your eyes will be affixed to the beads of sweat splattering off the top tube.

Little Cottonwood Canyon Road

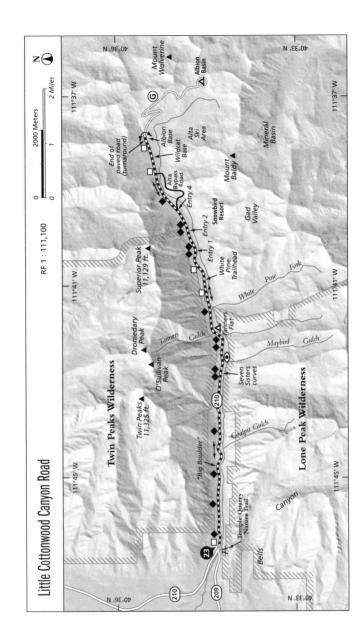

0.6 The smooth granite cliffs on the left are a rock climber's delight. They were the source rock for the construction of the Salt Lake Temple of the Church of Jesus Christ of Latter-day Saints in the 1800s, and today they provide safe storage for the church records.

1.0 There's a slight break in the grade, but you'll be pumping hard just the same.

1.6 The road tilts up to a strenuous grind as it passes a huge, precariously perched boulder on the left that always seems to be supported by a whimsical twig.

2.8 Pass the upper trailhead for the Little Cottonwood Canyon Trail and begin the steady grind up Seven Sisters curves. If you take a quick glance down the canyon, you'll see how an ancient glacier gouged the canyon into its classic U shape.

4.3 Pass Tanners Flat Campground, and the road rises steeper still to 9 percent. Ouch! The north side of the road is bound by a 3,000-foot-tall wall of rock notched by avalanche-ravaged ravines. The south side of the canyon, however, harbors long, deep, hanging valleys where smaller glaciers poured into the main trough.

4.8 The road widens to two lanes uphill, and the grade slackens a bit. Spin and recover.

5.4 Pass the White Pine Trailhead.

6.1 Pass Entry 1 at Snowbird Resort (Gad lifts), and the road resumes its crushing grade.

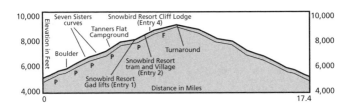

6.5 Pass Entry 2 at Snowbird Resort (tram and Village). This is where the Snowbird Hill Climb officially ends, but you still have 2 miles to claw away at, so keep chugging.

6.9 Pass Entry 4 at Snowbird Resort (Cliff Lodge and Alta Bypass Road). The road's unrelenting steepness might wear your psyche thin and make your legs revolt. The white and charcoal gray marbles of the Hellgate Cliffs stand in stark contrast to the layered tan and dark brown sedimentary rocks that surround them.

7.8 Pass the upper junction for the Alta Bypass Road. Skiers driving up to Alta on an epic powder day must take the detour to avoid the infamous Superior avalanche zone. Superior Peak towers overhead.

8.0 Keep pumping hard past Alta's Wildcat base, pass Rustler Lodge, and then make your sprint for the finish.

8.5 Pass the entrance to Alta's Albion base.

8.7 Reach the end of the paved road and the turnaround point. High fives! You rule! Read the interpretive plaque describing Alta's mining boom years while you recover, and enjoy the sights of treeless peaks that seal off the basin in all directions.

17.4 Arrive back at the flashing billboard.

24 Sego Lily Drive Loop

One of Sandy City's many designated bike routes, Sego Lily takes you on a casual jaunt through cheery residential areas in central Sandy. Although the route follows roads that receive moderate traffic, the wide shoulders and low speed limits provide a good margin of comfort. The loop is hardly epic, but that's the point. It's just a nice spin through the neighborhood. And since it passes two city parks along the way, and two more a couple blocks away, it's a good choice if you're towing the kids in a trailer.

Start: Dewey Bluth Park, Sandy.
Distance: 8.1-mile lariat-shaped loop.
Gain: 480 feet.
Physical difficulty: Easy. Except for two short, moderate hills, the loop is a piece of cake with gentle grades throughout. Freewheeling down Sego Lily Drive is payoff for your effort.
Margin of comfort: Good. Sego Lily Drive is a designated bike route with a shoulder of 4 to 6 feet, but the shoulder also doubles as a parking lane. The rest of the route follows residential roads that have wide shoulders and are proposed to become designated bike routes.
Season: March through November or throughout winter if the roads are dry and you can brave the cold.
Maps: USGS 1:24,000: Draper and Midvale, Utah.

Finding the trailhead: The loop begins at Dewey Bluth Park in Sandy, which is accessed off Sego Lily Drive/9800 South at about 200 East. (Parking is limited to two hours.) The entrance is between the UTA Trax line and Cascade Park Drive/230 East (private lane).
Know before you go: You must share the road with motorists throughout this route, so ride attentively. Be alert to vehicles exiting driveways and to doors being opened on parked cars.

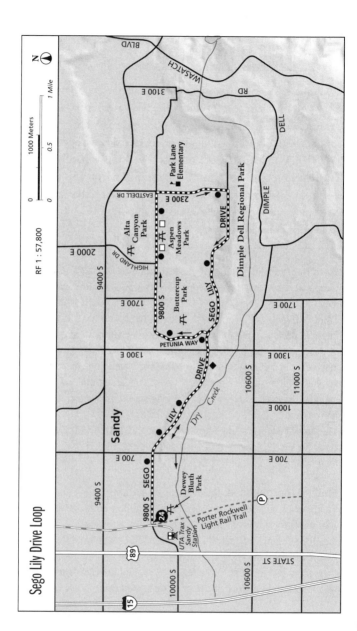

Sego Lily Drive Loop

RF 1 : 57,800

The Ride

The Sego Lily bike route officially begins at the Jordan River Parkway Trailhead on 10000 South and about 800 West, but the few miles from there to Dewey Bluth Park follow busy streets, cross railroad tracks, and pass under Interstate 15. You don't miss much by skipping that section.

0.0 From Dewey Bluth Park go right/east on Sego Lily Drive, which is a designated bike route. Little Cottonwood Canyon is dead in your sights, with Twin Peaks rising on the left and Lone Peak towering to the right.

0.6 Cross 700 East. The shoulder now doubles as a parking lane. Climb steadily but gently through a neighborhood of 1960s ranch-style houses.

1.8 Pump hard up a short, steep hill. Cross 1300 East and continue on Sego Lily Drive.

2.0 Turn left onto Petunia Way, officially leaving the Sego Lily bike route. You'll return on Sego Lily Drive later.

2.2 Cross Buttercup Drive at the Sandy Library and weave through a residential area. The road becomes 9800 South as it bends right/east.

3.2 Cross Highland Drive and begin the route's toughest climb—a moderately steep, 0.4-mile hill past Aspen Meadows Park. It's not that tough, but it will get your heart pumping.

3.9 Turn right onto Eastdell Drive/2300 East and breathe a sigh of relief because the climbing is done.

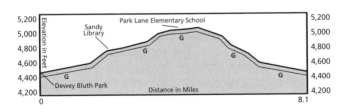

4.2 Cross 10000 South at Park Lane Elementary School and resume the bike route.

4.7 Turn right onto Sego Lily Drive and continue along the bike route. Pedal no more because you can coast all the way back to the trailhead. Whee!

6.2 Cross Petunia Way and follow your tracks back to the start.

8.1 Arrive back at Dewey Bluth Park. Now wasn't that fun?

25 Dimple Dell Loop (Draper)

Bust out this loop during lunch break or whenever you need a quick amp-out, and you'll return feeling it was time well spent. After a gradual spin out of Draper, you'll face a 0.8-mile-long wall up Wasatch Boulevard and then keep pumping up smaller inclines to Little Cottonwood Canyon Road. If you attack with gusto, you'll peg your anaerobic threshold and keep it there for twenty minutes or more. Reward for your effort is the thrilling descent around tight curves on Dimple Dell Road followed by easy miles on a country-style lane. If you lift your eyes from your cyclometer, you'll find the route first curves through an upscale residential community and then past pastures and horse ranches.

Start: Hidden Valley Shopping Center, Draper.
Distance: 12.3-mile lariat-shaped loop.
Gain: 700 feet.
Physical difficulty: Moderate. Although this ride is not long, there is one burly climb on Wasatch Boulevard—a 0.8-mile-long, 7 percent hill that will put the hurt on novice riders. The rest of the route rolls across gentle and moderate hills.

Margin of comfort: Fair to good. Wasatch Boulevard is a designated bike route with a wide shoulder and partial bike lane. The shoulder is less than 1 foot on Little Cottonwood Canyon Road, but the section is short. There is no shoulder on Dimple Dell Road, and although the road is narrow, traffic is relatively light.

Season: March through November or throughout winter if roads are dry and you can bear the cold.

Maps: USGS 1:24,000: Draper, Utah.

Finding the trailhead: The ride log begins at Hidden Valley Shopping Center at the corner of Draper Parkway (12300 South) and 1300 East. The loop portion of this route is commonly added onto the Wasatch Boulevard ride.

Know before you go: Traffic is moderate to heavy on 1700 East coming out of Draper, so ride cautiously and defensively. Know your handling skills and your bike's limits when descending the high-speed curves on Dimple Dell Road. You'll reach near highway speeds instantly if you let off the brakes.

The Ride

0.0 Begin at Hidden Valley Shopping Center at the corner of 12300 South and 1300 East. Go east on Draper Parkway, which curves north and becomes 1700 East. The shoulder is less than 1 foot for 0.6 mile, then widens to 4 feet. You'll warm up with a gradual climb.

1.2 Turn right onto Wasatch Boulevard. The road is one of Sandy's designated bike routes. Lone Peak towers high overhead.

2.1 Settle into your groove and start the long straightaway grind up the "wall," which rises at nearly 8 percent.

2.9 The grade lessens as the road bends north and passes Hidden Valley Park and the Church of Jesus Christ and Latter-day Saints.

3.1 Get back to work as the road angles uphill again. Welcome a slight respite, then roll northward across the Wasatch foothills.

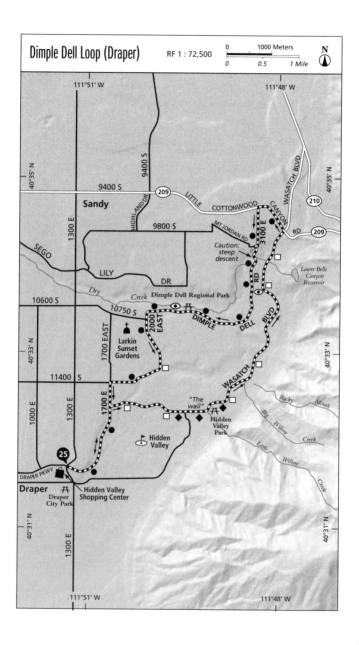

Dimple Dell Loop (Draper)

RF 1 : 72,500

0   1000 Meters
0   0.5   1 Mile

N

111°51' W

111°48' W

40°35' N

9400 S

9400 S

WASATCH BLVD

Sandy

209

LITTLE

COTTONWOOD

210

HIGHLAND DR

9800 S

MT JORDAN RD

3100 E

CANYON

RD

209

1300 E

Caution:
steep
descent

Lower Bells
Canyon
Reservoir

SEGO

LILY

DR

Dry

Creek

Dimple Dell Regional Park

10600 S

10750 S

DIMPLE

DELL

BLVD

40°33' N

2000 EAST

Larkin
Sunset
Gardens

1700 EAST

40°33' N

11400 S

WASATCH

Rocky

Mouth

1000 E

1300 E

1700 E

"The wall"

Hidden
Valley
Park

Big

Willow

Creek

Little

Willow

Hidden
Valley

Creek

25

DRAPER PKWY

Draper

Draper
City Park

Hidden Valley
Shopping Center

40°31' N

40°31' N

1300 E

111°51' W

111°48' W

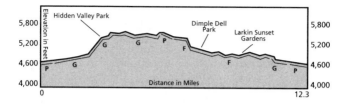

4.7 A series of short, moderate climbs take you onto the wide alluvial bench where the Little Cottonwood Canyon glacier once flowed into Lake Bonneville.

5.7 Turn left onto Little Cottonwood Canyon Road (9800 South) and breathe easy because the bulk of the climbing is done.

6.2 Turn left onto 3100 East at the Church of Jesus Christ of Latter-day Saints.

6.8 Bend right onto Mount Jordan Road (10010 South), then turn left immediately at the stop sign onto Dimple Dell Road (3050 East). Gravity takes hold quickly as you drop off the bench. How fast do you dare take the curves? (Stay in your lane and *do not* shortcut the curves!) Resume pedaling across the lowlands and pass horse ranches edging Dimple Dell Park. This section has a country-lane charm to it.

9.3 Immediately after Dimple Dell Road curves 90 degrees left and becomes 2000 East, stay southbound at the junction with 10720 South and pass Larkin Sunset Gardens (cemetery) on the right. Descend a small hill to a four-way junction and turn right/west onto 11400 South.

10.8 Turn left onto 1700 East.

11.1 Return to the familiar junction with Wasatch Boulevard to close the loop, then cruise south on 1700 East back to Draper.

12.3 Arrive back at Hidden Valley Shopping Center.

26 Dimple Dell Loop (Sandy)

The goal of this ride is to connect biker-friendly Wasatch Boulevard with Sandy's Porter Rockwell Light Rail Trail. The former hugs the mountains' foothills beneath the mighty stance of Lone Peak, and the latter follows an inactive railroad corridor past residential backyards and open spaces. Granted, you'll have to brush shoulders with motorists on all but the rail trail segment, but wide shoulders provide a good margin of comfort. Creative bicyclists will find it easy to connect this ride with Wasatch Boulevard northbound, a variety of rides in Draper, and even routes to South and West Jordan.

Start: Dewey Bluth Park, Sandy.
Distance: 14.5-mile loop.
Gain: 900 feet.
Physical difficulty: Moderate. The only hill of any consequence is the mile-long grind up 9400 South from Highland Drive to Wasatch Boulevard, which gains only about 400 feet. Before that you'll warm up nicely on gradual hills; thereafter, you'll coast and soft-pedal back to the trailhead.
Margin of comfort: Good. Wide shoulders (3 to 6 feet) border most of the roads, although traffic can be moderate to heavy. The shoulder on 9400 South narrows to less than 3 feet. Wasatch Boulevard is a designated bike route. The Porter Rockwell Light Rail Trail is a paved, nonmotorized recreation path.
Season: March through November and throughout winter when roads are dry and you can brave the cold.
Maps: USGS 1:24,000: Draper and Midvale, Utah. (Pick up Sandy City's free Parks & Trails Maps as well.)

Finding the trailhead: The loop begins at Dewey Bluth Park in Sandy, which is accessed off Sego Lily Drive/9800 South at about 200 East. The entrance is between the UTA Trax line and Cascade Park Drive/230 East (private lane).

Know before you go: Portions of the loop receive moderate to high traffic, so be aware of motorists, ride in single file, and stay as far right as possible. Parking at Dewey Bluth Park is limited to two hours. If you need more time, park at the UTA Trax lot at 115 East Sego Lily Drive.

The Ride

0.0 From Dewey Bluth Park go right/east on Sego Lily Drive, which is a designated bike route. In the distance Little Cottonwood Canyon is dead in your sights, with Twin Peaks rising to the left and Lone Peak towering on the right.

0.6 Cross 700 East. The shoulder now doubles as a parking lane. Climb steadily but gently through a neighborhood of 1960s ranch-style houses.

1.8 Pump hard up a short, steep hill. Cross 1300 East and continue on Sego Lily Drive.

2.0 Turn left onto Petunia Way, officially leaving the Sego Lily bike route.

2.2 Cross Buttercup Drive at the Sandy Library and weave through a residential area. The road becomes 9800 South as it bends right/east. The road is a proposed bike route.

3.2 Turn left onto Highland Drive and pass Alta Canyon Park.

3.8 Turn right onto 9400 South.

4.3 Cross 2300 East. The road curves right, and you begin a steep, half-mile-long climb up onto the east bench.

5.4 Cross 3100 East, and the grade mellows. The shoulder narrows to less than 1 foot for the next half mile. **Option:** To cut

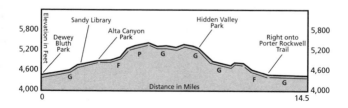

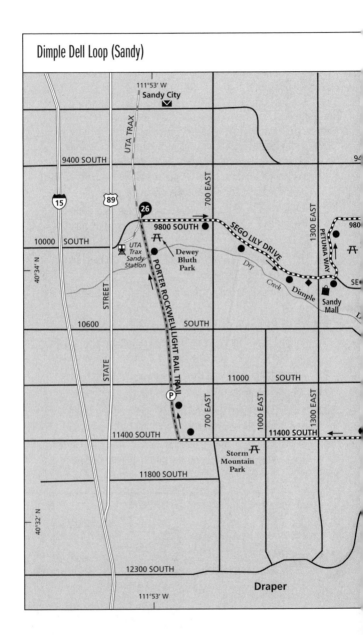

Dimple Dell Loop (Sandy)

Sandy City
111°53' W

UTA TRAX

9400 SOUTH

94

15

89

26

700 EAST

1300 EAST

980

PETUNIA WAY

9800 SOUTH

SEGO LILY DRIVE

10000 SOUTH

UTA Trax Sandy Station

Dewey Bluth Park

Dry

Creek

Dimple

SE

40°34' N

STREET

Sandy Mall

PORTER ROCKWELL LIGHT RAIL TRAIL

L

10600

SOUTH

STATE

11000

SOUTH

700 EAST

1000 EAST

1300 EAST

P

11400 SOUTH

11400 SOUTH

Storm Mountain Park

11800 SOUTH

40°32' N

12300 SOUTH

Draper

111°53' W

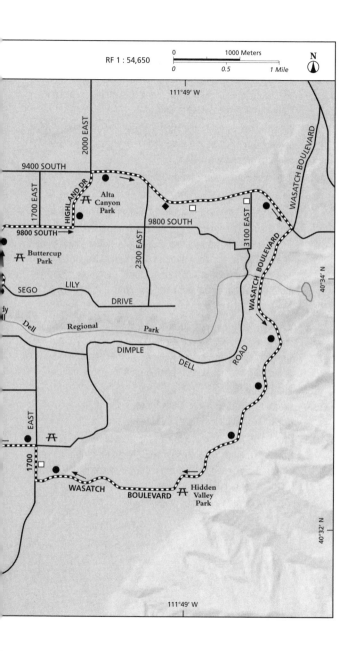

RF 1 : 54,650

0   1000 Meters
0   0.5   1 Mile

N

111°49′ W

2000 EAST

9400 SOUTH

1700 EAST

HIGHLAND DR.

WASATCH BOULEVARD

Alta
Canyon
Park

9800 SOUTH

9800 SOUTH →

3100 EAST

Buttercup
Park

2300 EAST

WASATCH BOULEVARD

40°34′ N

SEGO   LILY

DRIVE

dy   Dell   Regional   Park

DIMPLE

DELL   ROAD

WASATCH BOULEVARD

EAST

1700

WASATCH   BOULEVARD   Hidden
Valley
Park

40°32′ N

111°49′ W

this ride about 1 mile short, turn right onto 3100 East and loop past Dimple Dell Park to 11400 South.

5.9 Turn right onto Wasatch Boulevard. The road, a designated bike route, rolls up and down along the foothills with Lone Peak looming over your left shoulder.

8.6 Wasatch bends right near Hidden Valley Park, and you'll pick up speed quickly as the road descends a near 8 percent straightaway. Tuck and glide.

10.3 Turn right onto 1700 East and climb a short hill.

10.6 Turn left onto 11400 South.

11.2 Cross 1300 East. A sign warns of a steep downhill ahead, and you'll pick up speed quickly. The road widens to five lanes, and traffic can be heavy during weekdays—less so on weekends. The shoulder doubles as a parking/right turn lane. Watch out for drivers getting out of parked cars and for motorists approaching from behind wanting to turn right.

12.1 Cross 700 East.

12.5 Turn right onto the Porter Rockwell Light Rail Trail at the railroad crossing and leave the gas-guzzlers behind. (The trail is simply marked with a bike route sign.) The bike path runs peacefully past residential backyards and across undeveloped open spaces.

13.0 Cross 11000 South. Motorists have to stop at the train tracks, so you have a safe crossing.

13.5 Cross 10600 South, which is five lanes wide and heavily traveled. There is no stop sign or stoplight for motorists here, so you are advised to take the sidewalk to the intersection of 700 East and 10600 South and cross at the stoplight.

14.5 Arrive back at Dewey Bluth Park.

27 Draper Loop

Ask ten bicyclists how they ride the Draper Loop and you'll likely get ten different answers. This core loop leaves open several options for shortening or lengthening your ride. It's a simple ride on city streets starting at Draper City Park, linking to the Pony Express Road (Interstate 15 west frontage road), making a beeline through Sandy, and looping back to Draper. At under 15 miles it's a good ride for lunchtime or whenever time is short and you want to stretch your legs. You'll find sweeping vistas of the valley early in the ride before being immersed in traffic. The last leg runs along the Wasatch foothills beneath the watchful gaze of Lone Peak.

Start: Draper City Park, Draper.
Distance: 14.2-mile loop.
Gain: 700 feet.
Physical difficulty: Moderately easy. The loop has only two climbs: the long, gradual pull up Highland Drive and the short, steep grunt up 11400 East between 1000 East and 1300 East. The latter tilts up at nearly 8 percent grade, but it's barely a half mile long and thus is of little consequence.
Margin of comfort: Fair. The shoulder on most roads is 2 feet or more, and all roads receive at least moderate traffic, plus you must cross several busy intersections—all par for the course for riding in the Salt Lake Valley. 11400 South is a tight pinch where it crosses under I-15, as there is no shoulder there.
Season: March through November and throughout winter whenever roads are dry and you can brave the cold.
Maps: USGS 1:24,000: Draper and Midvale, Utah. (Some roads are not shown.)

Finding the trailhead: Begin at Draper City Park. From I-15 take exit 291 for 12300 South/Draper. Drive 2 miles east and turn right

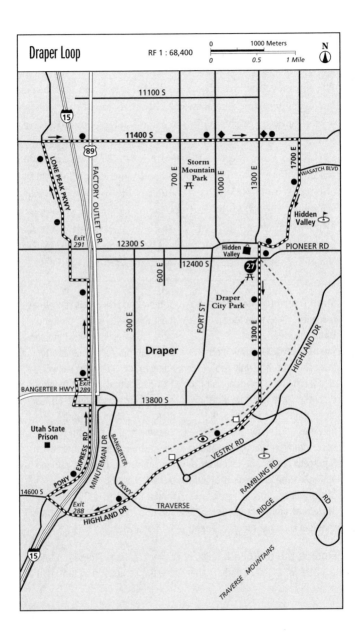

onto 1300 East, go through the roundabout, and turn right into Draper Park.

Know before you go: Other than Pony Express Road, which receives light traffic, all roads on this loop receive moderate to heavy traffic. Also, you must cross many busy intersections, so ride cautiously. Draper City Park has an outhouse, water tap, playground, and picnic pavilion. It also serves as trailhead for the Porter Rockwell Light Rail Trail, so while you hammer, your spouse and kids can lollygag on the easy-rated paved trail.

The Ride

0.0 From Draper City Park head south on 1300 East (bike lane). Recent construction in the southbound lane has damaged part of the bike lane; therefore, you might be forced to ride in the traffic lane where pavement is smoother.

1.5 Go under the railroad bridge, turn right onto Highland Drive, and climb gradually.

1.7 Pass Rambling Road forking left. As Highland Drive levels you'll find the entire Salt Lake Valley stretching beneath you all the way north to downtown Salt Lake City. The lofty Wasatch Range marks the eastern boundary of the Basin and Range Province, and the Oquirrh Mountains are the first in an echelon of north-south-trending mountains that characterize the landscape between Utah and California.

3.6 Climb moderately and cross Bangerter Parkway on the right and Traverse Ridge Road on the left at a stoplight. A

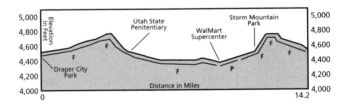

fast descent at 8 percent grade leads to the intersection with Minuteman Drive and to the I-15 interchange at 14600 South. Be alert to traffic entering and exiting the highway.

4.6 After crossing under I-15, turn right onto Pony Express Road (west frontage road). Ride past the Utah State Penitentiary and alongside I-15. Although there is no shoulder, traffic is light and the margin of comfort is fair.

6.3 Bend left around the "Pen," cross Bangerter Highway at a stoplight, and head north on 200 West, but then take the first right turn to continue on Pony Express Road.

7.7 Turn left onto 12650 South, then right onto Lone Peak Parkway. If you miss the left turn, you'll come to a dead end on Pony Express Road.

8.3 Cross 12300 South at a stoplight and continue north on Lone Peak Parkway. Initially there is no shoulder, but after a half mile the shoulder is a comfortable 3 feet.

9.5 Turn right onto 11400 South, kitty-corner to the new Wal-Mart Supercenter. 11400 South begins as a narrow two-lane road with no shoulder, then the road pinches to a tight squeeze where it crosses a small bridge and then passes under I-15. Pavement can be rough on this stretch as well, so watch your line and watch for traffic.

9.9 Cross State Street and pass a busy commercial area.

10.6 Cross the old railroad tracks where Sandy's Porter Rockwell Light Rail Trail heads north to Dewey Bluth Park. 11400 South widens to five lanes, and traffic can be heavy, but the shoulder/parking lane is 6 feet wide.

10.9 Cross 700 East. **Bail-out:** Although traffic is heavy on 700 East, it's a good choice to return to Draper because the shoulder is wide. This shortens the loop by about 1.2 miles, and you'll avoid the stiff climb ahead.

11.4 Cross 1000 East at Storm Mountain Park and gear down. Pump hard up the half-mile-long, 8 percent hill. The ride has been a piece of cake thus far, so go full throttle and make this effort count.

11.9 Cross 1300 East and top out of the climb. (1300 East is not a bicycle-friendly road, as it has no shoulder and traffic is heavy. It's a poor choice to return to Draper.) Although the now level road allows you to recover, you'll remain breathless by the awesome sight of Lone Peak towering overhead. 11400 East narrows to a two-lane road and traffic volume diminishes.

12.4 Turn right onto 1700 East.

12.7 Cross Wasatch Boulevard (left).

13.4 The shoulder disappears where 1700 East bends right, so be alert to traffic.

13.9 Turn left onto 1300 East and descend a small hill. Use caution crossing traffic to reach the left-turn lane.

14.2 Enter and exit the roundabout and arrive back at Draper City Park.

28 Traverse Mountains Loop

The combined climb up Rambling Road and Traverse Ridge Road is the main attraction, or distraction, of this ride. It's perfect for racers-in-training or for anyone wanting to build power in his or her pedal stroke. A fast glide into Utah County and long rolling miles around Point of the Mountain round out the loop.

Want scenery? This loop is stuffed with eye candy, from panoramic views of the Salt Lake and Utah Valleys, to inspiring vistas of the central Wasatch Range and Oquirrh Mountains, to shockingly beautiful sights of the southern Wasatch Range, including the formidable Mount Timpanogos. Not even the blight of two major gravel pits at Point of the Mountain can erase such indelible images of northern Utah.

Start: Draper City Park, Draper.
Distance: 24.5-mile loop.
Gain: 2,000 feet.
Physical difficulty: Moderately strenuous. Without much of a warm-up, you'll tackle the loop's main feature: back-to-back 6 to 8 percent climbs up Rambling Road and Traverse Ridge Road to Suncrest Drive. You'll gain nearly 1,700 feet over the first 6.4 miles. Reward for your effort is a speedy, swooping descent off the mountain followed by long, easy, rolling miles around Point of the

Mountain back to Draper.
Margin of comfort: Poor to fair overall. Many of the roads through Draper have bike lanes or wide shoulders, but the shoulder on Traverse Ridge Road and Suncrest Drive is about 2 feet, and traffic, including large trucks, buzzes by at fast speeds. Highway 92 is heavily traveled but the shoulder is 4 to 6 feet. The crux of the ride is the frontage road past Point of the Mountain, which can be unnerving for bicyclists, to say the least. Both the east

and west frontage roads are tight two-lane roads with no shoulders, and both provide access to major gravel pit operations. Large trucks motor quickly along these roads and pose a significant hazard for bicyclists. *Ride cautiously and defensively!*

Season: March through November and throughout winter when roads are dry and you can brave the cold.

Maps: USGS 1:24,000: Draper, Jordan Narrows, Lehi, and Midvale, Utah. (Some roads are not shown.)

Finding the trailhead: Begin at Draper City Park. From Interstate 15 take exit 291 for 12300 South/Draper. Drive 2 miles east and turn right onto 1300 East, go through the roundabout, and turn right into Draper Park.

Know before you go: As mentioned above, both the east and west frontage roads around Point of the Mountain are dangerous for bicyclists because of narrow traffic lanes, no shoulders, and large trucks accessing gravel pit operations. Bicyclists have been hit by vehicles on these roads in the past. This loop is safest on Sundays when gravel pits are closed. Still, these roads demand extreme caution. Likewise, portions of Traverse Ridge Road and Suncrest Drive are tight for motorists and bicyclists, and you might encounter large trucks accessing construction sites. *Use caution and ride defensively!*

The Ride

0.0 From Draper City Park head south on 1300 East (bike lane). Recent construction in the southbound lane has damaged part of the bike lane; therefore, you might be forced to ride in the traffic lane where pavement is smoother.

1.5 Go under the railroad bridge, turn right onto Highland Drive, and climb gradually.

1.8 Turn left onto Rambling Road for the South Mountain Golf Course. If you need a longer warm-up, then stay on Highland Drive to its intersection with Traverse Ridge Road, but why postpone the inevitable? Rambling Road tilts up to

Traverse Mountains Loop

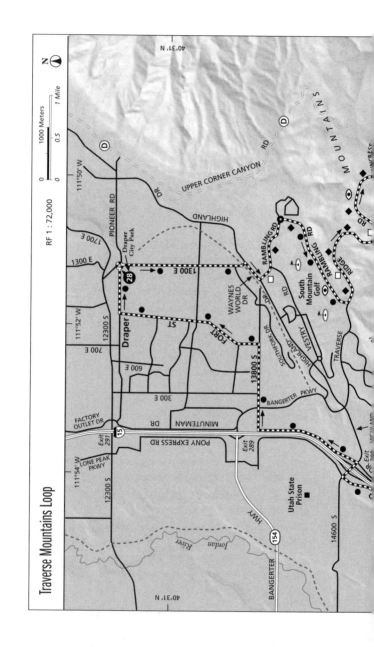

RF 1 : 72,000

0   0.5   1 Mile
0   1000 Meters

N

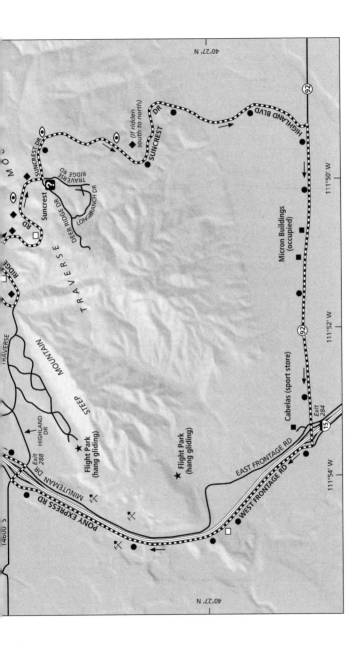

nearly 8 percent immediately, levels a touch, then angles up again for a steady pull. There is no white line but the two-lane road is wide and comfortable. Quickly you rise above the Salt Lake Valley onto the conspicuous ancient Lake Bonneville shoreline.

2.6 Turn right onto Mike Weir Drive at the roundabout and continue climbing steeply.

2.9 As the road bends west, it levels, and you'll find inspiring views of the entire Salt Lake Valley. Straight ahead on the distant Oquirrh Mountains, the massive tailing piles of Kennecott's Bingham Canyon Copper Mine sit where a mountain peak once stood.

4.2 Turn left onto Traverse Ridge Road (14600 South) and take a deep breath, for now the climb really begins. The road angles uphill quickly, levels briefly, then locks in at nearly 8 percent grade as it makes a huge horseshoe curve around a broad hollow. The shoulder is only 2 feet, so be alert to traffic. With the route swinging eastward, be sure to lift your head to gaze at the tall Gothic-like granite columns of Lone Peak's upper cornice. As the road turns southward and angles up a degree more, drop your nose to the handlebars and pump at full power. Work it!

6.4 Come to a four-way stop next to the Suncrest Visitor Center. If you're just into this ride for the hill climb, then turn around here (you'll find snacks and drinks at the Suncrest Market); otherwise, turn left onto Suncrest Drive, take a quick peek at Lone Peak in Salt Lake County and at Box Elder Peak in Utah County, and then tuck-and-glide down the short, steep

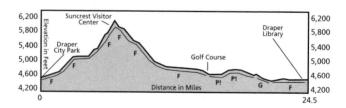

hill. Spin across the flats and tuck-and-glide again off the south side of the mountain around arcuate turns. Although the descent invites a hurried pace, the colossal view of Mount Timpanogos will nearly stop you dead in your tracks. American Fork Canyon cuts a deep, shadowy gash into Timp's base and Utah Valley stretches south, hemmed between the southern Wasatch Range and Utah Lake. The shoulder is only 2 feet, and may be littered with debris from trucks entering and exiting nearby construction sites, so ride cautiously.

9.9 Exit the foothills, roll onto the treeless flats, and resume pedaling on what is now Highland Boulevard.

11.5 Turn right onto Highway 92 and cruise along the flats. Traffic can be heavy on the two-lane highway. Be alert for turning vehicles as you ride through intersections for Micron and other roads.

14.1 Start descending to the I-15 interchange. You have just over a half mile to decide whether to ride the east or west frontage road around Point of the Mountain to Draper. The east frontage road can be more hectic than the west frontage road. Traffic can be moderate to heavy accessing Cabela's mega sports store, and as you round the Point and pass the gravel pit entrances, the two-lane road narrows drastically with a berm edging the right shoulder and a fence lining the left shoulder. You must ride in the traffic lane, and it's downright frightening if you get pinched by traffic here. The west frontage road is only slightly more comforting. It too is narrow and lacks a shoulder, but that's the way this loop is going.

14.9 The east frontage road forks right. Continue straight and pass under I-15, using *extreme caution* when crossing entrance and exit ramps.

15.2 Turn right onto Pony Express Road (west frontage road) at the intersection with Club House Road (Thanksgiving Point Golf Course). There is no shoulder, so ride cautiously and brace yourself for gravel trucks rumbling by.

16.5 Gear down for a short, steep incline that takes you up onto the bench. It's a sneaky way to add another hundred feet of vertical to your day.

17.1 Top out of the climb and cross the Utah/Salt Lake County line. Pedal on the flats and then enjoy a welcome coast.

19.5 Turn right onto 14600 South and go under I-15 (exit 288). Again, be alert to traffic entering and exiting the interstate highway.

19.8 Turn left/north onto Minuteman Drive, and find comfort in the designated bike lane.

21.3 The road bends right and becomes 13800 South. Cross Bangerter Highway and then 300 East.

22.1 Turn left onto Fort Street (745 East) and pick up another bike lane through the residential area.

23.9 Turn right onto Pioneer Road (12400 South). Traffic is generally light. To eliminate the last 0.2 mile of near shoulderless road and to avoid the roundabout, duck into the Draper Library parking lot and cut through to Draper Park.

24.5 Arrive back at Draper City Park.

29 Draper-Herriman Loop

"Once upon a time" this classic loop took bicyclists along quiet country roads to the remote reaches of the Salt Lake Valley, where cattle grazed and horses galloped through pastures to challenge the peloton. Today the Draper-Herriman loop follows the same roads, but farm fields are forever yielding to suburban sprawl and the once peaceful roads are now busy thoroughfares to designer neighborhoods. It's still a classic ride, but if you haven't pedaled out this way in years, you'll be shocked at the change.

Beginning in Draper, you'll head west to the foot of the Oquirrh Mountains, where Kennecott's Bingham Canyon Copper Mine turned a majestic peak into the world's largest hole. As you turn back east, the Wasatch Range stares you down, with Lone Peak growing more majestic with each pedal stroke.

Start: Draper City Park, Draper.
Distance: 25.1-mile loop.
Gain: 1,250 feet.
Physical difficulty: Moderate. With the lack of any significant hills on this loop, you can spin at a strong tempo on long flats and gentle inclines. The toughest climb checks in at about 2 percent grade, and that's nothing to sweat about.
Margin of comfort: Fair overall. Bike lanes run along 1300 East in Draper, Minuteman Drive/east frontage road, and 12600 South/12300 South from Riverton to Draper.
Season: March through November and throughout winter when roads are dry and you can brave the cold.
Maps: USGS 1:24,000: Draper, Jordan Narrows, Lehi, and Midvale, Utah.

Draper-Herriman Loop

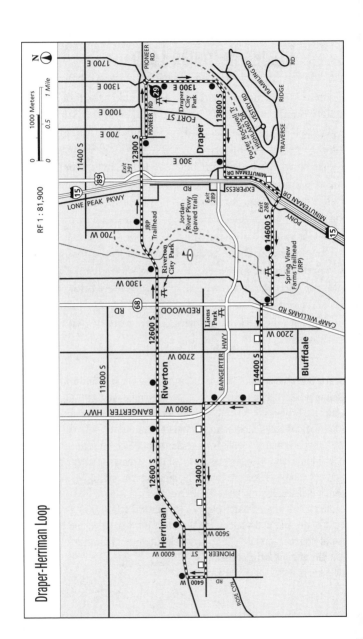

Finding the trailhead: Begin at Draper City Park. From Interstate 15 take exit 291 for 12300 South/Draper. Drive 2 miles east and turn right onto 1300 East, go through the roundabout, and turn right into Draper Park.

Know before you go: As the southwest corner of the Salt Lake Valley continues to expand, you'll see increased traffic now and in the years to come, so expect to share the road.

The Ride

0.0 From Draper City Park head south on 1300 East (bike lane). Recent construction in the southbound lane has damaged part of the bike lane; therefore, you might be forced to ride in the traffic lane where pavement is smoother.

1.4 Turn right onto Waynes World Drive, which bends right again and becomes 13800 South. The shoulder is about 1 foot, so be alert to traffic and ride defensively.

3.4 Turn left onto Minuteman Drive/east frontage road (bike lane). The road rises gradually then moderately, allowing your legs to warm up.

4.8 Come to the intersection with Highland Drive at exit 288 for I-15. Turn right, cross under the interstate, and head west on 14600 South. Watch out for vehicles entering and exiting I-15 at the interchange.

6.1 14600 South bends right and passes under the railroad tracks. Heed the stop sign, as the road narrows to one lane and the ensuing curve is blind. Drop off the bench into the Jordan River floodplain.

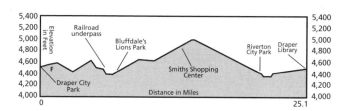

6.6 Pass the Spring View Farms Trailhead for the Jordan River Parkway (water and restroom). The shoulder is 1 foot. The road is a tight squeeze for vehicles and bikes, but traffic is generally light. The Draper suburbs yield to dispersed homes mixed with ranch lands and farm fields.

7.2 The road bends right/north and becomes 1690 West.

7.4 The road bends left/west and becomes 14400 South. Cross Camp Williams Road/Highway 68, and pass Bluffdale's Lions Park on the right, which can serve as an alternate trailhead. **Bail-out:** For a 14.2-mile ride, take Highway 68 north (becomes Redwood Road) and then 12300 South east to Draper.

9.4 The road bends right/north at 3600 West. The shoulder is now absent. Eastward you'll find a nice view of the Wasatch Range. From this angle you can see Box Elder Peak and Mount Timpanogos in Utah County plus Lone Peak in Salt Lake County.

10.6 Turn left/west onto 13400 South. The shoulder is absent.

10.9 Come to a stoplight at Bangerter Highway. Stay westbound. Now traffic is moderate and the speed limit is 40 mph. The shoulder is 1 foot and the lane is tight. If you haven't been out this way in a few years, then you'll be shocked at how Bluffdale and Herriman have grown as a result of suburban sprawl.

13.1 Cross Rosecrest Road (5600 West) at the Smiths Shopping Center. (You can take 5600 West north to 12600 South to shortcut the loop.)

14.2 Turn right onto Rose Canyon Road (6400 West).

14.6 Turn right onto Main Street (13100 South) in Herriman, now heading east on the loop's "back nine." (Turn left/west onto 13100 South to access Highway 101 along the Oquirrh Mountains foothills.) Traffic is light, making for comfortable riding.

17.1 As you cross 4570 West and enter Riverton, the shoulder pinches to less than 1 foot, so be alert to traffic and ride cautiously. The road bends and becomes 12600 South.

18.0 Cross Bangerter Highway at a stoplight. Eastward on 12600 South you'll pick up the wide bike lane. Although you must contend with high-speed traffic, the margin of comfort is fair to good.

20.4 Cross Redwood Road. Again traffic is heavy on 12600 South, but you have a nice wide bike lane to ride in.

20.7 Pass Riverton City Park at 1450 West (alternate trailhead). Lone Peak is dead in your sights, rising to stately proportions and flaunting granite columns in its upper cirque.

21.7 Enter the Draper city limits and pump quickly up a hill rising out of the Jordan River floodplain. The road jogs and becomes 12300 South.

22.8 Cross Lone Peak Parkway. If you started the loop from Riverton, then take Lone Peak Parkway right and to 14600 South, instead of heading into Draper.

23.0 Cross under I–15 at the very busy interchange. You still have a bike lane through here, but be alert to traffic when crossing entrance and exit ramps.

23.9 Turn right onto 600 East. (The bike lane continues on 12300 South to 1000 East, but then it disappears. Riding on 12300 South between 1000 East and 1300 East is dangerous, as there is no shoulder.)

24.0 Turn left onto Pioneer Road (12400 South). Caution! This is a two-way stop and traffic on Pioneer Road does not stop!

24.9 Pass Draper Library. The shoulder pinches to less than 1 foot for the remaining 0.2 mile. You can ride on the sidewalk or duck into the library and ride through the parking lot to access Draper City Park.

25.1 Enter the roundabout at 1300 East, go right, and arrive back at Draper Park.

30 Camp Williams Loop

A gravel pit, an Army training grounds, and a state penitentiary. What more could you want? How about mighty views of Lone Peak and Mount Timpanogos in the Wasatch, inspiring sights of the Oquirrh Mountains, and wind-rippled farm fields surrounding the rural hamlet of Lehi? Now we're talking. You'll find all of these on the Camp Williams Loop. This fast-paced, scenic tour on the southernmost end of the Salt Lake Valley has been a road biker's standard for decades.

Start: Riverton City Park, Riverton.
Distance: 27.3-mile loop.
Gain: 900 feet.
Physical difficulty: Moderate. Two gradual climbs, the first past Point of the Mountain and the second past Camp Williams, are of little consequence. More arduous might be battling a headwind on these flat, open roads.
Margin of comfort: Fair overall. 12600 South has a bike lane, and the shoulder on Redwood Road north of Camp Williams is 3 feet or more. Lone Peak Parkway, the frontage road past Point of the Mountain, Thanksgiving Way, and residential roads through Lehi do not have shoulders, but traffic is generally light to moderate. The shoulder on Highway 73 west of Lehi and on the first 3 miles of the Camp Williams Road/Highway 68 is less than 1 foot and traffic can be heavy; use caution.
Season: March through November and throughout winter when roads are dry and you can brave the cold.
Maps: USGS 1:24,000: Jordan Narrows and Midvale, Utah.

Finding the trailhead: Start at Riverton City Park at 1450 West on 12600 South. Take exit 291 off Interstate 15 for 12300 South/Riverton and travel 2.4 miles west (12300 South becomes 12600 South).

Know before you go: Parts of this loop have narrow or no shoulders with moderate to heavy traffic, so ride cautiously and defensively. You can reload on water and food in Lehi.

The Ride

0.0   From Riverton City Park at 1450 West on 12600 South, take the bike lane east on 12600 South and descend into and climb out of the Jordan River floodplain. Lone Peak, rising over a mile above the valley floor, is dead in your sights, and Mount Timpanogos pokes its head above the Traverse Mountains.

2.0   Turn right onto Lone Peak Parkway before the I-15 underpass, and then go left onto 12650 South.

2.6   Turn right onto Pony Express Road, which is the west frontage road to I-15. The shoulder is less than 1 foot but traffic is light.

3.9   Turn left onto 200 West and cross Bangerter Highway at the stoplight.

4.3   Go left/east at a T-junction toward a sign for Lone Peak correctional facility and circle around the state penitentiary.

5.7   Cross 14600 South near the I-15 interchange to continue on Pony Express Road/west frontage road. A park-and-ride lot here is an alternate starting point. Climb gradually and steadily around Point of the Mountain. If the wind is out of the north, you'll likely see hang gliders soaring in the thermals from the Point's north Flight Park. The shoulder is

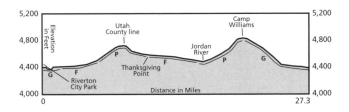

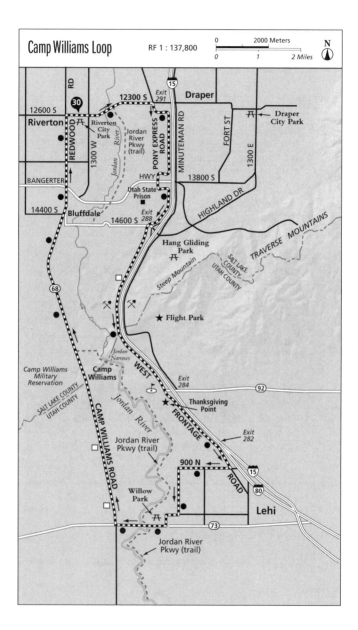

Camp Williams Loop

RF 1 : 137,800

0   2000 Meters

0   1   2 Miles

N

RD

30

12300 S

Exit 291

Draper

12600 S

Riverton

Riverton City Park

Draper City Park

REDWOOD

1300 W

Jordan River

Jordan River Pkwy (trail)

PONY EXPRESS ROAD

MINUTEMAN RD

FORT ST

1300 E

BANGERTER

HWY

13800 S

Utah State Prison

14400 S

Bluffdale

14600 S

Exit 288

HIGHLAND DR

Hang Gliding Park

TRAVERSE MOUNTAINS

68

Steep Mountain

SALT LAKE COUNTY

UTAH COUNTY

★ Flight Park

Jordan Narrows

Camp Williams Military Reservation

Camp Williams

WEST

Exit 284

92

SALT LAKE COUNTY

UTAH COUNTY

Jordan River

★ Thanksgiving Point

FRONTAGE

Exit 282

CAMP WILLIAMS ROAD

Jordan River Pkwy (trail)

900 N

15

ROAD

80

Willow Park

Lehi

73

Jordan River Pkwy (trail)

absent on the frontage road, so ride cautiously. And watch out for dump trucks accessing the gravel pit operations west of the road. You'll find a good view of the southern Oquirrh Mountains foothills to the west. You'll ride across them shortly.

8.3 Cross the Utah County line at the low-lying pass. Mount Timpanogos rises majestically above Utah Valley, and Mount Nebo, the tallest peak in the Wasatch at 11,928 feet, sculpts the southern horizon. Tuck-and-glide down a steeper hill on the south side of the pass. If the wind is out of the south, then you'll find hang gliders hovering off the Point's south slopes.

10.2 Go through the stoplight onto Thanksgiving Way.

10.8 Pass Thanksgiving Point. Glance left and you'll find a marvelous sight of Mount Timpanogos. Cock your head even farther to view up Dry Creek Canyon between Box Elder and Lone Peaks.

12.0 Pass exit 282 off I-15, then go through a stop sign at 1870 North and continue south on Trinaman Lane through quiet neighborhoods. (Alternatively, you can cross over onto U.S. Highway 89 and take it into Lehi.)

13.2 Turn right onto 900 North. The shoulder is absent. You'll ride on paved farm roads for the next 3 miles and skip busy US 89 into Lehi.

14.9 The road bends left/south at 2395 West. Pass more ranches and pastures on the quiet lane.

15.5 Just before the road bends left/east, turn right/west onto an unsigned paved road.

15.8 Bend left at the entrance to Willow Park.

16.1 Intersect Main Street/Highway 73 and turn right/west. The shoulder is 1 foot and the speed limit is 55 mph, so ride cautiously and hold your line.

16.6 Cross the Provo-Jordan River Parkway.

17.3 Turn right/north onto Camp Williams Road/Highway 68 at the Smiths Shopping Center. Over the next 3 miles, the margin of comfort is poor, as the two-lane road is tight, traffic can be moderate to heavy, and the shoulder is less than 1 foot. Again, ride cautiously. Farm fields and pastures in the foreground frame the towering Wasatch peaks. The road rises gradually and steadily for 3 miles.

20.7 The road levels and passes the entrance to the Army National Guard's Camp Williams then begins descending gradually.

24.8 Cross 14400 South at a stoplight and continue north on Highway 68, which is now Redwood Road.

27.0 Turn right onto 12600 South and pick up the bike lane.

27.3 Arrive back at Riverton City Park.

31 Jordan River Parkway

Running from Utah Lake through the heart of the Salt Lake Valley to Davis County, the Jordan River Parkway (JRP) offers pedestrians, joggers, in-line skaters, and bicyclists a safe, peaceful, scenic, and natural recreational retreat from the confines of urbanism. The river itself is a natural waterway by which Utah Lake drains into the Great Salt Lake. Inasmuch, its floodplain harbors wetlands and groves of ancient cottonwoods that attract an array of birds and small animals. It's not a wildlife preserve or national park, and there are many reminders that the trail runs through a metropolis: Residential developments huddle along the river's banks, busy roadways cross the path, and industrial centers are in close view. Still, the numerous parks, picnic areas, and playgrounds passed along the way make the trail an invaluable asset to the entire community.

Start: Various locations at about 1200 West between Bluffdale and North Salt Lake.

Distance: Varies: the Parkway is 26.2 miles with some gaps.

Gain: 200 feet from north to south or -200 feet from south to north.

Physical difficulty: Easy. Except for one small blip on the southernmost section, which rises a meager 30 vertical feet, the trail is as flat as a pancake. In fact, the average grade is only 0.3 percent, which is virtually unnotice-

able in the bicycling world.

Trail surface: Paved, nonmotorized, multi-use trail. There is a half-mile dirt stretch between 3900 South and 3300 South and a 2-mile dirt stretch north of 1000 North.

Season: March through November and throughout winter whenever the trail is dry and you can brave the cold.

Maps: USGS 1:24,000: Jordan Narrows, Midvale, Salt Lake City South, and Salt Lake City North, Utah.

Finding the trailhead: There are twenty-three major trailheads, most of which have restrooms and water taps. Some parks have picnic areas, playgrounds, and other amenities. You might be able to access the JRP from additional locations.

Know before you go: The JPR is not a race course, so leave your heart rate monitor at home. Be alert and courteous to other users, especially to families with children. Stay to the right side of the trail and slow down at curves. The trail and parks close at 11:00 P.M., and dogs must be leashed. Use caution crossing roads where there is not an underpass or a crossing signal. Nearly thirty years in the making, the JRP is still discontinuous. Riding the entire trail means taking often busy city streets around incomplete sections.

Goatheads! A curse on mountain bikers, the spiky seeds from this small sprawling plant are found randomly along the JRP. Most appalling is their propensity to gang up on you: If your tires pick up one, they will likely have picked up several. Don't pull them out right away, as the pin-size holes are difficult to locate and patch. You may be able to ride back to the trailhead without flatting or with only a slow leak. Using tire liners or tube sealants is *highly* recommended; otherwise, carry multiple spare tubes and a dozen or more patches.

The Rides (from the south with existing gaps)

#1. 14600 South to 12300 South: 9.8 miles out and back.

> **0.0** From the Spring View Farms Trailhead (14600 South), the trail curves northward through the willow brushes.

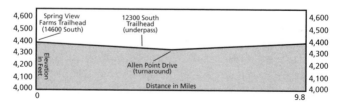

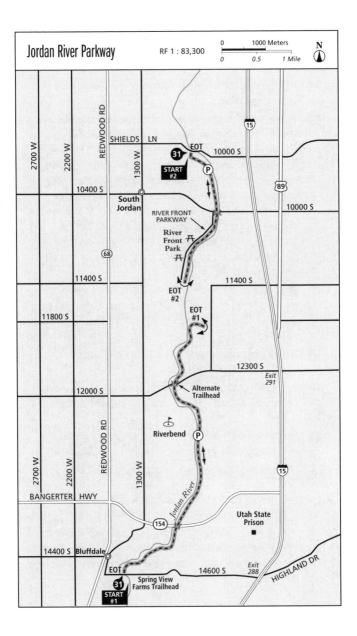

Jordan River Parkway

RF 1 : 83,300

0   1000 Meters
0   0.5   1 Mile

N

2700 W

2200 W

REDWOOD RD

SHIELDS LN

1300 W

31
START #2

EOT

10000 S

15

89

10400 S

South Jordan

RIVER FRONT PARKWAY

10000 S

River Front Park

68

11400 S

EOT #2

11400 S

EOT #1

11800 S

12000 S

12300 S

Exit 291

Alternate Trailhead

Riverbend

P

2700 W

2200 W

REDWOOD RD

1300 W

15

Jordan River

BANGERTER HWY

154

Utah State Prison

14400 S   Bluffdale

EOT

14600 S

Exit 288

HIGHLAND DR

31
START #1

Spring View Farms Trailhead

0.4 Reach the junction with Spring View Farms Trail, which accesses a new residential community. Stay northbound on the JRP, crossing bridges over canals.

0.6 Reach the junction with Madison River Trail forking east; cross a footbridge.

1.5 Attack the JRP's one and only hill, as the trail rises abruptly out of the river bottom. Give your riding buddies your best "Lance glance" and make your breakaway move, charging up the grade and laying the peloton to waste. When you near the top, pop out of the saddle and pump even harder to confirm who is the boss. As Lance once learned against Marco Pantani, there should be no gifts, so crest to the top decisively. Okay, so Alpe d'Huez this is not; the climb is barely 30 vertical feet, not 3,000. By the time you start panting, you're over the top and rolling back down into the river plain at an idle cruise.

2.8 Wind through the weedy wetlands. To the east Lone Peak and Twin Peaks guard over Little Cottonwood Canyon; to the southeast Mount Timpanogos pokes its head above the Traverse Mountains.

3.5 Pass a footbridge accessing Riverbend Golf Course and cross under 12300 South.

3.8 Reach the 12300 South Trailhead. Continuing north, the JRP crosses open spaces and offers a long view of the Wasatch Range.

4.9 The trail currently ends at Allen Point Drive (trail access but no trailhead parking). Turn around here.

9.8 Arrive back at Spring View Farms trailhead (14600 South).

#2. 10000 South to 11400 South: 4.8 miles out and back.

0.0 Start at the 10000 South Trailhead on the south side of the road and head *south,* following the river's west bank. (There is no point going north because the trail ends shortly after the 10000 South underpass.)

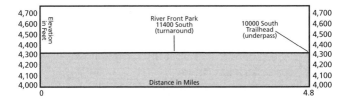

- **1.0** Cross under 10600 South and pass behind Neumont University and other commercial developments.

- **1.7** Reach River Front Park. This half-mile-long greenbelt park has picnic areas, pavilions, volleyball courts, and playgrounds.

- **2.4** The JRP ends abruptly in the grass next to River Front Parkway at about 11400 South. Currently, there is no connection between here and the trailhead on 12300 South. Turn around here.

- **4.8** Arrive back at 10000 South.

#3. 7800 South to I–80: 29.6 miles out and back.
This stretch of continuous trail serves as a model for green-belt park projects throughout the nation. Developed city/county parks are passed every couple of miles at major street crossings, and underpasses provide safe crossings of those busy streets.

- **0.0** From the 7800 South Trailhead, ride south for a couple hundred feet and cross the footbridge to the right, then circle back north and go under 7800 South. (The trail also continues south for 1.3 miles before ending at 700 West at about 8500 South.) Head north past the outhouse, riding between the river on your right and the railroad tracks on your left. (You can access Gardner Village on the north side of the underpass.) The trail splits twice; both routes rejoin shortly.

- **1.9** Cross under 6400 South and enter Murray's Winchester Park. The trail curves playfully along the stream's bank and offers a great view of the Wasatch Front. The trail splits several times, making small loops. Stay to the right and along the river's west bank, following the dotted yellow line; explore the side paths on your return. The Murray-Parkway Golf Course lies across the river.

2.4 Cross a bridge to the river's east bank. (The path continues on the west bank but ends shortly at a residential area.)

2.6 Cross under Interstate 215. The trail splits but rejoins. Stay to the right/east, and explore the other lanes on the return.

3.1 Come to the parking lot for Cottonwood Grove on Murray Parkway Avenue/1080 West. Cross Bullion Street/5820 South (crosswalk) and enter Walden Park. The trail continues on the river's east bank and runs behind residences. Interpretive signs along the way explain the river's habitat and the history of pioneers who settled along the river's edge.

3.7 Come to Walden Park's main parking area on 5400 South, which has a pavilion and playground, and then cross under 5400 South. Enter Germania Park on the north side of 5400 South. Stay to the right/east on the main path.

4.2 Come to the Germania Park pavilion. Stay right/east, following the dotted yellow line. The left/west lane turns to dirt shortly, but rejoins the main paved trail farther north. Pass the trailhead parking lot near Lucky Clover Lane and cross a wooden boardwalk over the river's marshy oxbows.

5.5 Curve past Arrowhead Park on the south side of 4800 South and go through the underpass. North of 4800 South the trail travels along the river's west bank.

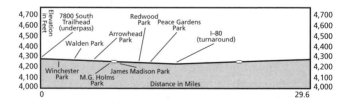

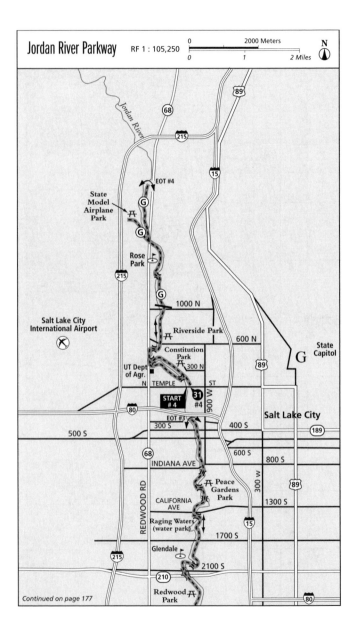

Jordan River Parkway

RF 1 : 105,250

0   2000 Meters
0   1   2 Miles

N

Jordan River

89

68

215

15

EOT #4

State
Model
Airplane
Park

G

G

Rose
Park

G

215

1000 N

Salt Lake City
International Airport

Riverside Park

600 N

State
Capitol

G

Constitution
Park

300 N

89

UT Dept
of Agr.

N   TEMPLE

ST

START
4

31
#4

900 W

Salt Lake City

80

EOT #3

300 S

400 S

189

500 S

600 S

68

INDIANA AVE

800 S

REDWOOD RD

CALIFORNIA
AVE

Peace
Gardens
Park

300 W

1300 S

89

Raging Waters
(water park)

15

1700 S

215

Glendale

210

2100 S

Continued on page 177

Redwood
Park

80

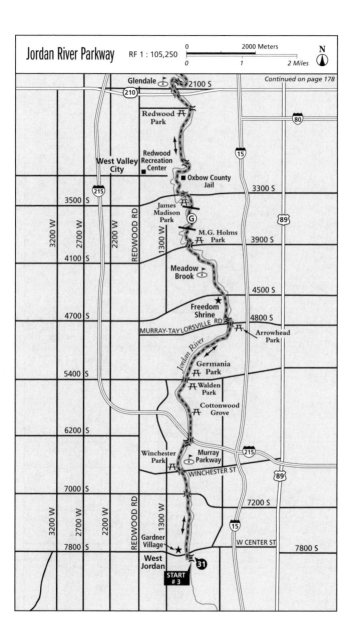

Jordan River Parkway

RF 1 : 105,250

Continued on page 178

N

Glendale — 2100 S
210
Redwood Park
West Valley City
Redwood Recreation Center
80
15
Oxbow County Jail
3300 S
215
3500 S
James Madison Park
G
89
M.G. Holms Park
3900 S
4100 S
Meadow Brook
4500 S
4700 S
Freedom Shrine
4800 S
MURRAY-TAYLORSVILLE RD.
Arrowhead Park
Jordan River
Germania Park
5400 S
Walden Park
Cottonwood Grove
6200 S
Winchester Park
Murray Parkway
215
WINCHESTER ST
7000 S
89
7200 S
15
W CENTER ST
Gardner Village
7800 S
7800 S
West Jordan
31
START #3

3200 W 2700 W 2200 W REDWOOD RD 1300 W

6.1 On the south side of 4500 South, the trail passes the Freedom Shrine. The memorial was created by the National Exchange Club to strengthen and to garner appreciation of our national American heritage. The arcuate wall displays replicas of key documents in America's history, including the Declaration of Independence, Constitution, Bill of Rights, "Star-Spangled Banner," Emancipation Proclamation, Martin Luther King's "I Have a Dream" speech, and the inaugural speeches of Washington, Jefferson, Lincoln, Kennedy, and others. Take a minute to brush up on your history and to reflect on our nation's foundation of freedom and democracy.

7.5 Cross 3900 South. There is no underpass, so you must cross the four-lane highway. Pass the M. G. Holms WW II Memorial Park on the north side of 3900 South. The paved trail turns to packed dirt and fine gravel. Tall cottonwood trees drape the trail, giving it a woodsy feel; then they part to reveal a long view of the Wasatch Front.

8.1 Dirt reverts to paved trail.

8.6 Wind past James Madison Park and cross under 3300 South. The trail makes a big horseshoe curve past the Oxbow Facility (county jail). Surprisingly, the tall trailside trees make this section especially pleasant.

9.5 Pass the small parking area for the Oxbow Trailhead and then cross a bridge to the river's west bank. The trail continues on the river's east bank too, but it runs behind warehouses. The west bank trail is more wooded.

9.9 Stay straight/north at two junctions signed for Redwood Center. If you fork left toward Redwood Center, you can make a little side loop to the main trail.

10.6 At the Redwood Trailhead stay on the river's west bank, although a footbridge allows you to cross the river and explore the path on the east bank.

11.0 Go under Highway 201 then under 2100 South.

11.2 Go right and cross a footbridge at Glendale Golf Course. Make a horseshoe bend south and then north and around the golf course. Follow bike route signs.

11.7 Wind through a small chain-link fence labyrinth that forces trail users to slow down for the railroad track crossing. Can you make it through the maze without dabbing a foot?

11.9 Cross 1700 South. The paved trail follows the west side of Riverside Drive (1125 West) with the river and a park on your left.

12.4 Cross a bridge to the west bank and then cross California Avenue (1350 South). The trail follows 1300 South for 0.3 mile, then curves away from the residential street to follow the river's wooded bank.

12.9 Enter a small park with a canoe ramp and stay left of the playground. Check out the small displays of tile mosaic artwork in the park, and then cross a footbridge to the river's east bank. Pass the Urban Treehouse pavilion, exit Bend in the River Park, and cross Fremont Avenue (crosswalk only).

13.4 Enter International Peace Gardens Park, but don't go all the way through it. Cross a footbridge to the river's west bank and follow alongside 1100 West.

13.6 Cross the railroad tracks and veer right to cross a footbridge to the river's east bank.

13.8 Cross Indiana Avenue (850 South).

14.1 Cross 700 South (crosswalk only) and check out the sculpture titled "Sphere" next to the Pioneer Police Precinct. The trail runs along the river's east bank (don't cross the bridge) and alongside Jake Garn Boulevard (1120 West).

14.3 Cross 500 South and muse at the sculpture titled "Prometheus Fire Bearing."

14.8 The trail ends at the tall embankment beneath Interstate 80. There is no crossing here, so turn around and retrace your tracks. **Option:** If you want to continue north, then you must take city streets around I-80. First head east onto 300

South, then go left/north onto 1000 West (bike lane). Cross North Temple Street (use caution at this busy intersection) and turn left onto 300 North (bike lane). Where 300 North curves right and becomes Clark Avenue (about 1200 West), enter Constitution Park and hook up with the JRP.

29.6 Arrive back at 7800 South.

#4. North Temple Street to the Davis County Line: 8.2 miles out and back.

Although this section officially begins at North Temple Street, there is no trailhead parking there, and pedaling along North Temple to access the JRP is dangerous because there is no shoulder. Instead, park and embark from Constitution Park on 300 North and about 1200 West.

0.0 The JRP intersects the sidewalk on North Temple Street and heads north on the river's east bank behind the Utah State Fairpark. (You can cross the bridge here or farther north.)

0.3 Pass Constitution Park on the right (preferred trailhead).

0.8 Cross a bridge to the river's west bank just north of the Utah Department of Agriculture building (alternate trailhead).

1.1 Cross 500 North (crosswalk only) and cross a bridge to the river's east bank.

1.6 Cross 700 North and ride next to residential backyards.

2.1 Come to 1000 North (crosswalk only). The paved path ends here. North of 1000 North the JRP is a dirt doubletrack, so it is only recommended for mountain bikes.

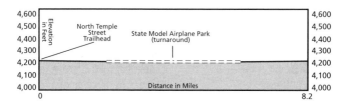

2.7 Ride through Rose Park Golf Course.

3.5 Use caution crossing Redwood Road. The trail on the river's west bank accesses the State Model Airplane Park. The trail on the river's east bank runs for another half mile to its end at the Davis County line near I-215.

4.1 Reach the turnaround.

8.2 Arrive back at North Temple Street.

32 West Jordan-Bluffdale Loop (the "Pen" Loop)

If you ask ten people how they ride around the "Pen," you'll likely get ten different answers. This loop attempts a reasonable north-south route between West Jordan and Riverton, taking in a variety of roads. It's a good fitness ride where you can spin, spin, spin. Although it's mostly flat, it's far from mundane because the sights of the central Wasatch Range are impressive and ever changing. Nearby the scene changes from residential to commercial to open spaces where livestock graze; sometimes you'll pass all three at once.

Make it a family day out, even if the rest of the family doesn't bike, as there is lots to do at West Jordan City Park: picnic areas, playgrounds, ball fields, and swimming (at the nearby Gene Fullmer Fitness Center).

Start: West Jordan City Park, West Jordan.
Distance: 24.1-mile loop.
Gain: 600 feet.

Physical difficulty: Moderate. Hills are mere blips on the greater Salt Lake bicycling radar. The steepest is the abrupt climb out of the Jordan River bottomlands up to 1300 West. It's steep but not more than two dozen pedal strokes.

Margin of comfort: Fair overall. The shoulder throughout the loop varies from 0 to 3 feet on average, and traffic is light to moderate depending on the time of day. There are no designated bike lanes.

Season: March through November and throughout winter whenever roads are dry and you can brave the cold.

Maps: USGS 1:24,000: Jordan Narrows and Midvale, Utah. (Some roads are not shown.)

Finding the trailhead: Begin at West Jordan City Park (1985 West and 7800 South). From Interstate 15 take exit 297 for 7200 South. Go west on 7200 South (becomes 7000 South) and turn left onto Redwood Road. Turn right onto 7800 South and enter the park on Veterans Memorial Parkway (1985 West).

Know before you go: Pavement on 1300 West can be cracked, broken, and patched, resulting in a rough ride for thin tires. Be sure to carry a spare tube and equipment to fix a flat. Likewise, these conditions might force you to ride in the traffic lane, so be aware of traffic at all times.

You can begin this ride from a number of different staging areas, including the Jordan River Parkway Trailhead on 7800 South, Midvale, Draper (access from 12300 South or 14600 South), and Riverton (Riverton City Park at 1450 West and 12600 South).

The Ride

0.0   From West Jordan City Park, exit the park to 7800 South, pick up the bike lane heading east, and cautiously cross Redwood Road. After crossing 1300 West, the designated bike lane ends but the shoulder is 4 to 6 feet. At the railroad underpass near Gardner Village, the shoulder disappears briefly, so be aware of Traffic approaching from behind. Pass the Jordan River Parkway Trailhead on the right (alternate staging area) and enter "old town" Midvale.

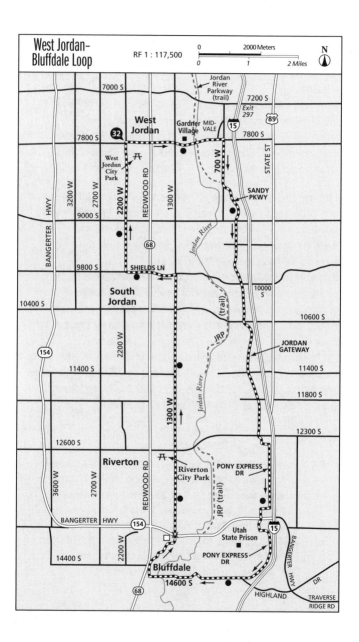

West Jordan–Bluffdale Loop

RF 1 : 117,500

0   2000 Meters
0   1   2 Miles

N

7000 S

Jordan River Parkway (trail)

7200 S

Exit 297

West Jordan

Gardner Village

MID-VALE

7800 S

7800 S

32

STATE ST

15

89

West Jordan City Park

700 W

3200 W

2700 W

2200 W

REDWOOD RD

1300 W

SANDY PKWY

9000 S

68

Jordan River

BANGERTER HWY

9800 S

SHIELDS LN

10000 S

South Jordan

10400 S

154

(trail)

JRP

10600 S

JORDAN GATEWAY

2200 W

11400 S

11400 S

Jordan River

11800 S

1300 W

12300 S

12600 S

Riverton

3600 W

2700 W

REDWOOD RD

Riverton City Park

JRP (trail)

PONY EXPRESS DR

BANGERTER HWY

154

Utah State Prison

15

BANGERTER HWY

2200 W

PONY EXPRESS DR

DR

14400 S

Bluffdale

68

14600 S

HIGHLAND

TRAVERSE RIDGE RD

1.8 Turn right/south onto 700 West at the stoplight in the center of town. There is no white line, but the effective shoulder is 4 to 6 feet and doubles as a parking lane.

2.6 Just after passing the fire department, turn left onto Sandy Parkway/frontage road and pump hard for a dozen pedal strokes up a sharp but short hill. The road winds past commercial and industrial complexes, but the pavement is smooth and the road makes for pretty decent bicycling. Attack another slight hill, then relax.

3.5 Cross 9000 South and continue south on Sandy Parkway/frontage road. The shoulder pinches to zero at the intersection then widens to 5 feet. Some slight curves break up the monotony of riding on the flats.

4.8 Cross 10000 South. Views of the central Wasatch Range are fine, and Twin Peaks on the Cottonwood Ridge and Lone Peak on the Alpine Ridge are most prominent. The Traverse Mountains, which separate Salt Lake County from Utah County, are straight ahead down the road.

5.6 Cross South Jordan Parkway/10600 South, and the frontage road becomes Jordan Gateway/325 West. It makes a dogleg left, crosses the railroad tracks, and then bends right.

6.8 Cross 11400 South and continue spinning easily across open spaces blended with new housing developments. The Ebay headquarters is on the left, and you might find sheep grazing in nearby pastures. How's that for contrast?

8.0 Cross 12300 South, and the frontage road becomes Lone Peak Parkway. Jog left, then right, and turn left at the T-junction with 12650 South.

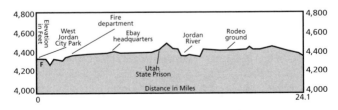

8.6   Turn right onto Pony Express Drive, which continues the I–15 frontage road. The shoulder narrows to less than 1 foot, but traffic is generally light. Still, be aware of motorists approaching from behind. Enjoy the brief but impressive view of Mount Timpanogos rising above the Traverse Mountains. As you continue south, the pyramid-shaped Box Elder Peak pokes its head around the shoulder of Lone Peak.

9.9   Go left at the T-junction with 200 West and cross Bangerter Highway at the stoplight.

10.6   Turn left at a T-junction, following the sign for the Lone Peak correctional facility, and then bend right to continue on Pony Express Drive. The shoulder is less than 1 foot.

11.4   Pass the entrance to the Utah State Prison, a.k.a. the "Pen"; thus the route's nickname. Don't pick up any hitchhikers!

11.8   Turn right onto 14600 South for Bluffdale next to the I–15 interchange. The shoulder is less than 1 foot, but traffic is light to moderate. Ride past small industrial sites and dispersed homes that share the rural lands with horses and cows grazing in sunny pastures.

12.8   Follow the cautionary arrows that steer you right at an intersection. The road makes an S bend, and you should heed the stop sign at the railroad underpass where the road narrows to one lane. Drop swiftly off the old bank of the Jordan River and glide across its broad floodplain, passing the Spring View Farms Trailhead for the Jordan River Parkway (restroom and water tap). Now the road has a country-lane feel to it.

13.9   14600 South bends right/north and becomes 1690 West.

14.1   The road bends left/west and becomes 14400 South, but don't make the bend. Go straight at the unsigned intersection onto what will eventually become 1300 West. If you come to the intersection with Redwood Road, you missed the turn by 0.1 mile. (Alternatively, you can return on Redwood Road.) The road passes farmlands and pastures that take advantage of the Jordan River's fertile bottomlands. If not for the towering Wasatch peaks across the valley, you might think you've been transported to New England's rolling countryside. There is no shoulder on this tight two-lane road, so you'll have to ride in the traffic lane, but there's rarely any traffic down here. Watch out for broken pavement and pot-holes edging the road and in your lane. Paris-Roubaix it's not, but it's a bumpy ride just the same. Hold your line and don't veer into the oncoming lane.

15.3 Make a sharp bend left and pump hard to rise quickly out of the river's bottomlands and back onto the valley floor. The road curves east, then north, and becomes 1300 West. There's no white line on 1300 West initially, and the road's edge is often broken and patched pavement. Point out haz-ards to your fellow cyclists, keep errant moves to a mini-mum, and be aware of traffic, which is generally light and slow. Modern residential developments, dispersed older homes, and grassy pastures maintain the ride's rural feel.

16.7 A small rodeo ground and ballpark mark the intersection with 12800 South. Go left here if you want to reach Riverton City Park (alternate staging area).

16.9 Cross 12600 South. Traffic volume increases from light to moderate. North of 12400 South there is a good amount of road damage and patched pavement in your lane, so you might be forced to ride in the traffic lane. Do so cautiously.

19.6 Cross 10400 South/South Jordan Parkway. Crest a small hill and pass the Jordan River Temple on the left.

20.4 Turn left onto Shields Lane (9840 South). The three-lane road offers ample room for bicycles and vehicles, plus the pavement is noticeably smoother. (Alternatively, you can con-tinue on 1300 West to 7800 South and retrace your tracks to West Jordan City Park.)

20.9 Cross Redwood Road, staying on Shields, and ride past resi-dences and open spaces.

21.4 Turn right onto 2200 West. Traffic on this two-lane road is generally light to moderate, so it's relatively biker friendly.

23.3 Cross Sugar Factory Road (8250 South) and pass the old sugar factory on the right, which is now the Sugar Factory Playhouse. Come alongside West Jordan Park, backed by a good chunk of the central Wasatch Range.

23.9 Turn right onto 7800 South and pick up the bike lane.

24.1 Arrive back at West Jordan City Park on Veterans Memorial Parkway (1985 West).

33 Oquirrh Mountains Loop

Completing a century ride is one of cycling's great achievements. You'll earn respect from your cycling peers, awe from those outside the cycling circle, and bragging rights you can tout for years. The Oquirrh Mountains Loop is a dead-on century laid out to perfection. The lack of any tough climbs and a total elevation gain of only 2,500 feet make this ride a realistic target for a greater number of cyclists seeking to break the 100-mile barrier.

You'll ride on moderately to heavily trafficked roads around the north end of the Oquirrh Mountains and down the length of the Salt Lake Valley. Although much of your attention will be focused on your front wheel and holding your line, there's immense eye candy when you lift your head, including panoramas of the Great Salt Lake and lengthy views of the Wasatch Front. Around the Oquirrh's south end and west side, you'll ride a backcountry highway across Utah's desolate western desert. Here, vast dirt and sagebrush prairies with nary a home in sight fill the void between lofty mountain ranges that announce the onset of the Basin and Range Province.

Start: West Jordan City Park, West Jordan.

Distance: 102-mile loop.

Gain: 2,500 feet.

Physical difficulty: Extremely strenuous; it's a century. Fortunately, there are no crushing climbs, just several long, steady efforts, like the 20-mile, 1,000-foot vertical rise from Lehi to Fivemile Pass. By and large, you can spin at high cadence throughout the ride.

Margin of comfort: Fair. The shoulder varies throughout the ride from nonexistent to generous. Trouble spots where the shoulder is minimal and the margin of comfort poor are south of Camp Williams Road on Highway 68, Highways 73 and 36 between Fairfield and Tooele, the short stretch on Interstate 80, sections of Highway 201 west of Magna, and parts of 3100 South. The margin of comfort along the rest of the route is fair to good, with the shoulder varying between 3 and 6 feet.

Season: March through November and throughout winter when roads are dry and you can brave the cold.

Maps: USGS 1:100,000: Salt Lake City and Tooele, Utah.

Finding the trailhead: Start at West Jordan City Park (1985 West and 7800 South). From Interstate 15 take exit 297 for 7200 South. Drive 1.5 miles west and turn left onto Redwood Road. Turn right onto 7800 South, then turn left into the park on Veterans Memorial Parkway.

Know before you go: This is a long ride, so be prepared physically and mentally. Carry adequate food and water and appropriate equipment and clothing. Be well stocked with water and food for the 37-mile stretch of lonely, empty highway between Cedar Fort and Tooele. On some sections of road, the shoulder is less than 1 foot and traffic is high speed. Use extreme caution on the short stretch of I-80, as intermittent rumble strips along the road's edge may force you to ride close to the white line and next to high-speed traffic.

Which way to ride this loop? Clockwise, as described, puts a gradual but long-winded climb in the loop's first half, and the margin of comfort is a tad higher. Counterclockwise, you'll face several

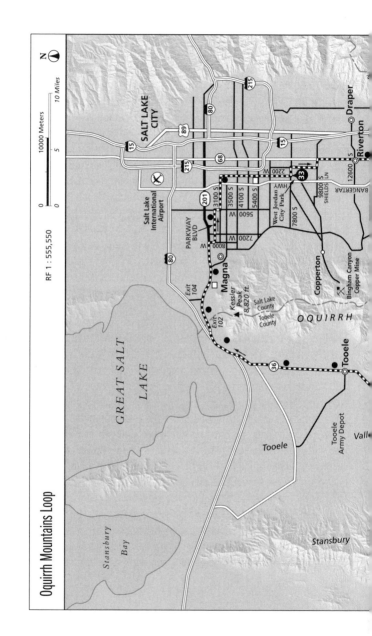

Oquirrh Mountains Loop

RF 1 : 555,550

N

0   5   10 Miles

0   10000 Meters

GREAT SALT LAKE

Stansbury Bay

SALT LAKE CITY

Salt Lake International Airport

PARKWAY BLVD

Magna

Kessler Peak 8,820 ft.

Salt Lake County
Tooele County

OQUIRRH

Copperton

Bingham Canyon Copper Mine

West Jordan City Park

Draper

Riverton

BANGERTAR

Tooele

Tooele Army Depot

Stansbury

Vall

Exit 104

Exit 102

3100 S
3500 S
4100 S
5400 S
5600 S
7200 S
7800 S
8000 W
7200 W
9800 S
SHIELDS LN
12600 S
2200 W

Tooele

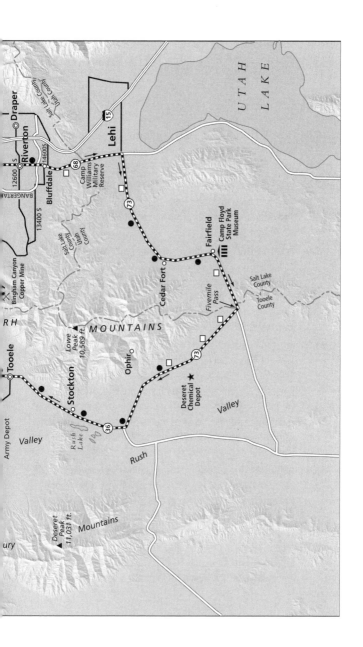

shorter, sharper climbs, but the view of the Wasatch Range coming off Fivemile Pass all the way into Lehi is a jaw-dropper. Try it both ways and decide for yourself.

The Ride

0.0 From West Jordan City Park, exit the park onto 7800 South, take the sidewalk west, and then turn left/south onto 2200 West. Traffic is generally light to moderate.

2.8 Turn left onto Shields Lane/9800 South.

3.2 Turn right onto Redwood Road/Highway 68. Redwood narrows from four lanes to two lanes and traffic can be moderate to heavy.

9.0 Cross 14400 South; Redwood Road becomes Camp Williams Road. Gradually you'll gear down as you begin the loop's first climb—a gentle 4-mile, 400-foot rise to the county line and past the entrance to Camp Williams. This effort will warm up your legs nicely. The shoulder gradually narrows to zero at the pass.

13.1 Crest the pass at Camp Williams and shift up for a fast descent. The shoulder is zero here and the two-lane road is a tight squeeze for bikes and vehicles, so use extreme caution. Basically, motorists won't be able to pass you without crossing into the opposing lane. If you lift your eyes off the road, you'll find a stunning view of the southern Wasatch Range rising above Utah Valley, with Utah Lake shimmering like an oasis.

16.3 Turn right onto Highway 73. Gas stations/convenience stores are at the intersection if you need to refuel. Except for the Cedar Valley Country Store in Cedar Fort 12 miles up the road, you won't find a drop of water until you reach Stockton, which is 40 miles away. That's if Penny's Cafe is open; otherwise, it's another 5 miles to Tooele. In short, you should be stocked up for nearly 50 miles of riding, and you'll be going uphill for the bulk of it. The road angles up at about

4 percent grade for several miles, levels, then tilts up again briefly. As the road bends gradually southwest, it moderates to a gentle but steady rise, and you can spin easily. The southern tip of the Oquirrh Mountains is off in the distance to the southwest. That's where you're heading.

27.7 Enter the hamlet of Cedar Fort. Stop into Cedar Valley Country Store and stock up on drinks and munchies because you're about to head out across no-man's land. The views of the southern Wasatch Range are stunning from this angle, with distant Mount Timpanogos rising above the more proximal Lake Mountains. A gradual but welcome downhill takes you south of Cedar Fort for a few miles.

32.2 The highway strikes westward at Fairfield and rises uphill again. History buffs can stop into the Camp Floyd Museum to experience life during the pioneer era. The Pony Express once rode through Fairfield on its way across northern Utah, and you'll trace its exact tracks up to Fivemile Pass. The shoulder narrows to less than 1 foot and will stay that way until Tooele. Although the 5-mile climb to Fivemile Pass gains only about 400 feet, it's exasperating.

37.0 Cross the Utah/Tooele County line at Fivemile Pass and sight across the hapless Rush Valley to the distant Sheeprock Mountains on the southwestern skyline. As the road wraps around the Oquirrh Mountains on their west flank, the Stansbury Mountains come into view and offer strong alpine motifs in the midst of the high-desert bleakness. Roll up and down and up and down along the highway.

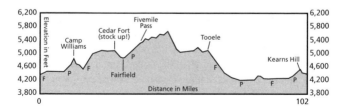

48.2 After passing the turnoff for the old mining camp of Ophir, the road bends west and descends directly. You'll have the wind in your face and a magnificent view of 11,031-foot-tall Deseret Peak square in your sights. If the sirens go off while you pass the Deseret Chemical Depot, you'd better hope there is a favorable wind; otherwise, you'll have only seconds to don the chemical suit and gas mask you remembered to pack in your jersey pocket. Didn't you?

52.8 Veer right onto Highway 36 and ride the flats into Stockton. If you're running on empty, you can stop into Penny's Truck Stop and Cafe, but the bikers you'll meet there wear leather, not Lycra. A gradual run-up takes you to the south end of Tooele and to the top of another long, welcome descent.

63.8 Tooele has it all: country cafes, fast food joints, even a brew pub. Watch your line as you ride through downtown because the shoulder is narrow and doubles as a parking lane. When you leave the north end of town, the road becomes five lanes. Pedaling is a breeze as you relish the gradual, 5-mile-long descent.

70.0 Hit the flats and resume pedaling at high tempo. Cattle find good grazing on the grasslands out here, and it's easy to make out the conspicuous shoreline bench that Lake Bonneville cut into the Oquirrh Mountains' foothills.

76.1 Come to the I-80 interchange. Watch out for cars and trucks at this busy commercial intersection. Follow the ramp onto I-80 east and merge with the interstate. This is a dicey stretch of highway, and the margin of comfort is poor. Intermittent rumble strips line the right edge of the shoulder, leaving you about 2 feet of smooth pavement right of the white line, and traffic whizzes by at 75 mph. Brace yourself for a blast of wind from passing semis, or ride the rumble strips to play it safe. Take in the view of the Great Salt Lake, Antelope Island and Stansbury Island, and the distant northern Wasatch Range, if you dare lift your eyes from your front wheel.

79.0 Round the north end of the Oquirrh Mountains and take exit 102 for Highway 201 and Magna. Rise up a small hill past Kennecott's copper smelting facility and coast down the other side. The shoulder varies and traffic on the four-lane highway is moderate to heavy and fast, so use caution. Pass the first exit for Magna and continue on Highway 201.

87.0 Get off Highway 201 at 8000 West. The two-lane road is tight and the shoulder is less than 1 foot, so use caution.

87.5 Turn left onto Parkway Boulevard. Initially, Parkway is biker friendly as it passes dispersed residences and grassy pasture. After crossing 7200 West, however, the shoulder narrows to less than 1 foot, but traffic is generally light.

90.5 Turn right onto 5600 West. The shoulder is less than 1 foot and traffic can be heavy on this narrow two-lane road; use caution.

91.1 Turn left onto 3100 South. This is a busy intersection surrounded by commercial businesses. You should have realized by now that you've left the open road and have reentered the realm of urban sprawl. Traffic is moderate on 3100 South, and the shoulder varies from 0 to 8 feet, so ride defensively.

94.1 Turn right onto 3200 West. Hope you have some legs left because the upcoming climb, although drawn out and just a tad over 1 percent grade, might be enough to nail your coffin shut. You'll battle constant traffic and cross several busy intersections on this last leg, so keep your head clear and ride cautiously.

98.4 Cap the climb atop Kearns Hill and take one last look at the Oquirrh Mountains, which you just circumnavigated. Cross 6200 South and savor a short stretch of freewheeling.

100.6 Turn left onto 7800 South.

102.0 Arrive back at West Jordan City Park. Phew!

Honorable Mentions

Here are some rides that missed the cut but are worthy of mention. No doubt there are a slew of other rides, too. Get out and ride, take some notes, and report back.

Liberty Park: Although the park's loop road is only 1.4 miles long and perfectly flat, Liberty Park is a magnet for cyclists and inline skaters. Traffic is one-directional (counter-clockwise) and speed limits are slow. If you're venturing into the world of cycling for the first time, Liberty Park is a great place to teach your legs to turn in circles. Enter Liberty Park on 600 East from either 1300 South or 900 South.

Sugarhouse Park: The 1.4-mile road around Sugarhouse Park makes learning to ride a bike exciting. The curvy road has two small climbs and two quick descents. Views of the central Wasatch Range are breathtaking. Head to the park for the annual Sugarhouse Criterium and watch the area's strongest riders race around the road in tight formation.

Rocky Mountain Speedway: Road racers head out to the drag strip for the weekly criterium race, and the speedway makes for a pretty decent ride from downtown anytime. Round trip distance is about 25 miles and it's virtually flat. Start at Liberty Park and go west on 800 South (bike lane). After passing under Interstates 15 and 215, turn left onto Pioneer Road, and then follow it west as it bends and becomes the Highway 201 north frontage road. Zigzag past industrial complexes and turn left onto 5600 West. Cross over Highway 201 and turn right onto the Highway 201 south frontage road to reach Rocky Mountain Speedway.

Bacchus Highway (Highway 111): Highway 111 along the Oquirrh foothills was a classic back when the west side of the valley was largely undeveloped. Today Highway 111 is fraught with heavy traffic, high speeds, and big trucks, all on the same old narrow two-lane highway with little shoulder. The highway is not biker friendly but still draws dedicated cyclists. Sunday is the best day to ride. To make a decent 30-mile loop, start at West Jordan City Park and follow the first leg of the Oquirrh Mountains Loop to 14400 South and then the Draper-Herriman Loop to Herriman. Stay west on 13100 South then curve north onto Highway 111 near Butterfield Canyon. Make a flat beeline north, then take New Bingham Highway (Highway 48) back to 7800 South and West Jordan Park.

Porter Rockwell Light Rail Trail: The easy 3.8-mile Porter Rockwell Trail starts at Draper City Park. The paved railroad grade makes a big arc through old and new neighborhoods and past horse pastures. Views of the Valley and surrounding mountains are superlative. Go as far as Bangerter Highway and then retrace your tracks to Draper Park.

11th Avenue: Although only 1.6 miles long, 11th Avenue is one of the city's most popular bike routes and a key connector between City Creek Canyon and the University of Utah area. For an easy 5.7-mile loop through the Avenues neighborhood, start at Memory Grove Park and ride the paved lane to City Creek Canyon. Go right onto Bonneville Boulevard to 11th Avenue. Take 11th Avenue eastbound (a slight incline) then turn right onto Virginia Street and descend to 3rd Avenue. Return to Memory Grove Park via 3rd Avenue (a slight decline).

About the Author

Gregg Bromka was bitten by the mountain biking bug when he reluctantly rode Moab's Slickrock Trail with his buddies in the mid-1980s. Since then Gregg has developed an obsession with Utah trails and has written more than a half-dozen guidebooks, the latest being *Mountain Biking Utah's Wasatch Front* and *Mountain Biking Park City & Beyond*. Road biking completes his love for pedaling two wheels.

A transplant from upstate New York and with a degree in geology, Gregg has made Salt Lake City his home for more than twenty years.